FISHING FLIES AND THEIR PLUMAGE

Fishing Flies
AND THEIR
PLUMAGE

MICHAEL VEALE
Foreword by Michael Shephard

· THE ·
SPORTSMAN'S
PRESS
LONDON

Published by The Sportsman's Press, 1989

British Library Cataloguing in Publication Data
Veale, Michael
Fishing flies and their plumage.
1. Fly fishing. Flies. Tying – Manuals
I. Title
688.7'912

ISBN 0-948253-39-8

Photoset and printed in Great Britain by
Redwood Burn Limited, Trowbridge, Wiltshire

Contents

Acknowledgements

My book would have been very difficult to complete without the help of a number of people, and firstly I would like to acknowledge the fly-tyers of the past whose writings have provided the foundations on which I developed my own fly-tying skills and knowledge.

My very special thanks go to Major Michael Shephard, MC, for reading my original handwritten manuscript and for his subsequent advice and encouragement, which in turn gave me the motivation to have it typed and look for a publisher.

My appreciation and thanks also go to the following: Gordon Bellman of Plymouth, who took the photographs with superb skill and with his infectious enthusiasm made the photo sessions a delightful experience; Carey L. Quarles, Ph.D., of Colorado Quality Hackles, Fort Collins, USA, for use of the information given and for the magnificent colour photograph of his range of cock capes which is reproduced in this book; Mike Summers for kindly allowing me to use his salmon patterns; Chris Martindale and David Clark of Liskeard, Cornwall, who tried out experimental fly patterns and kept me informed of the results; and Alan Bramley of Partridge Hooks, for supplying the hooks on which most of my patterns are dressed.

Finally, my very special thanks to my wife, Gwen, for her help in tying flies, looking after the poultry, and encouragement and support given over the years.

S. M. Veale

List of Illustrations

Foreword

Michael Veale's knowledge of the artificial fly is like the trunk of a tree whose roots are firmly secured in the experience and excellence of experts in our past, while its branches continually grow upwards into the unknown, discovering and bearing new fruits.

With his own expertise as a fly-dresser firmly based on the teachings of those who had attained their reputations around the turn of the century, it is not surprising that the disciple should soon acquire enough confidence to become a first-class copier of the well-established patterns: but it would have been entirely out of the character of the man I have come to know had he been content to remain in the shadow of those masters!

It is almost as though the apprentice of thirty years ago, having mastered the fundamental skills of his craft, saw ways to improve on the old perfections and embraced them with an enthusiasm which took him deep into the realms of experiment with both method and material. Whatever Michael Veale's views on various aspects of the art are today, the reader can be assured that they are founded soundly on practical application. After all, to obtain the best of feathers he set out to breed them himself to the standards he demanded while his fertile mind sought out substitutes for some materials now unavailable to the fly-tyer and alternatives with which he could improve on the performance of those commonly in use. The experiments go on and the patterns change with every year.

As I have said, the apprentice became an improver . . . not only as a craftsman, but as one who found ways to better what was currently accepted as the best! I recall an occasion when I asked Mike to produce for me copies of patterns immortalised by one whose name will ever remain in the Fly-Dressers' Hall of Fame. Producing the finished goods, my friend modestly told me that he had not actually copied the pattern, but had improved on it . . . and he had!

I shall always remember another commission when I asked him to reproduce W. C. Stewart's spiders of 150 years ago. I gave Mike the old lawyer's book, *The Practical Angler*, first published in 1857, and asked him to copy the three flies described by that great fisherman of the beautiful Border streams. Two of these called for the use of feathers no longer available (at least, I hope not) – from the outside wing of the landrail and from the dotterel. Mike found perfect alternatives commonly available and, for good measure, improved on Stewart's use of a starling feather (which was at hand) for the third spider!

That incident also had an amusing sequel. We wanted the patterns to illustrate an article in *Trout & Salmon*, after the publication of which a reader criticised the finished products as being 'too heavily dressed'. Now, we all know that the essential ingredient of a spider is sparseness in its dressing – a fact stressed by Stewart himself when condemning some of the flies sold in shops. We considered this comment and Mike said, 'Well, you cannot get a sparser hackle than one of one-and-a-half turns!'

Necessity, they tell us, is the mother of invention, but invention is really in Master Veale's blood and often stems from practical questions asked when fishing the rivers and pools of the West Country. A Cornishman, he has not – save for some years in the Royal Navy – spent much of his life far across the river Tamar: but his knowledge of his trade knows no borders and the assistance this can give his fellow fly-tyer and brother angler will extend across the oceans.

Michael Shephard MC
Altarnun,
Cornwall.

Introduction

Over the years I have experimented with various combinations of materials with the view of producing the perfect fishing fly. Some of my attempts have produced one-day wonders, others have proved effective and have stood the test of time. Therefore I am compiling a record of my most successful patterns and how best to fish them. I consider these patterns to be as original as they can be. I am not aware if there are any patterns with the same dressing and name; it is possible, I suppose, that there could be some duplication of dressings that may have been devised years ago, and I have simply re-invented them. I have included standard dressings and my variations of them, with dressings from other tyers that I know to be effective on West Country waters.

This book in the main deals with fly patterns and materials to dress them. To introduce the reader to the fly-dressers' art, I list a few of the tools and materials required; however it is by no means a complete list, just enough items to start the beginner on the way. I take the reader through each stage of tying a fly and hopefully this will give some idea of how it is done: the easy way of learning is to go to fly-tying classes, or a fishing course. An hour's instruction from an experienced tyer is worth more than a book full of words.

I give tying tips on some of my dressings when required; these tricks of the craft will make the tying of some patterns considerably easier. Firstly and foremost, quality must be the aim as there is no point spending money on materials, and time tying, if the end product falls apart after a couple of casts.

1

The Beginning

I first started fly-fishing for sea trout in the mid 1950s, and bought my flies from a little shop in a Cornish town called Lostwithiel. The flies were very well tied and I remember that sea trout flies dressed on a size six wide gape hook cost me a shilling [5p] each. In my first season I found how effective the Alexandra pattern was, and it has probably been my favourite ever since; certainly in its various modes it has lured more fish into my landing net than any other fly.

In the early 1960s I started to take an interest in fly-dressing and the materials used. I soon discovered that for wet fly hackles the plumage of game and water birds were far superior to those of poultry. The beauty of water or gamebird hackles is their mobility in the water, particularly the way life is imparted to the artificial fly. The barred and speckled appearance of hackles with the superb range of colours ensures they have no equal in fly dressing. I take a lot of my hackles, particularly the small sizes, off the wings of game birds. I use grey mallard or teal quills for the dry fly winging.

Some fly-tying books give starling hackles or wings quills in many dressings. Personally I do not like starling as I consider it is far too soft and delicate. A fly dressed with starling feathers ends up after a couple of fish, or a careless back cast dragged through the vegetation, just a body on a hook with no hackle or wings.

For the perfect dry fly hackle, I kept my own poultry and bred for quality and colour with success. Probably there cannot be many fly-tyers who have taken an egg from under a hen, then made up a nest with a 'broody' and taken a trout on a fly dressed with a hackle from a cock that was hatched out of that nest. I go into the keeping and breeding of poultry for their plumage later in the book.

All the flies listed are proven and suitable for rivers and lake fishing, and will take brown, rainbow, sea trout and salmon. It is possible to tie them on virtually any size hook, however for trout a size four should be considered the largest. If a long fly is required use a longshank hook, two hooks in tandem, or a normal fly with a flying treble hook (a flying treble is the term given to a size 14 or 16 treble hook joined by a piece of nylon line to the hookshank on which the fly is tied). When dressing the fly, make sure the tail and wing is long enough to mask the treble; the extra length will improve the appearance and effectiveness of the pattern, and hides the sting in the tail.

Although it is possible to tie flies holding the hook in the fingers and the only tool required is a sharp pair of scissors, to start with I would recommend the following tools are acquired:

Flyting vice
Pair of good quality scissors
Pair of hackle pliers
A dubbing needle

Razor blade
Bobbin holders.

The most expensive item of the tools is the vice. There are many types of fly-tying vices available so I would suggest a middle range model which will take hook sizes from small trout fly hooks up to medium salmon sizes. Look for a vice which has slim jaws, thus enabling small flies to be tied as there will be no bulk of metal to interfere with the tying operation. A quality vice will have a good broad-based clamp to ensure a sound anchor fixture to the work top. Make sure the vice jaws can be rotated so that double and treble hooks can be dressed, and so the fly can be inspected from every angle.

In my view a bobbin holder is essential as it holds the spool of tying silk, and it does away with the need for half-hitches at the end of every tying stage. Its weight is adequate to hold in place any materials tied in.

Hooks   There are a vast range of different types for the fly-tyer to choose from. For my patterns the sizes are based on the 'Redditch' scale, and in the main I use only 'Partridge' wide gape or longshank hooks.

Silks   For many years the most widely used tying silk was 'Pearsall Gossamer', but there are now a host of nylon threads available, some of them pre-waxed. I have no special preference but the pre-waxed threads are more convenient.

Rayon floss   A very good body material, it can be split for the smaller sizes. I like using rayon as the colour will darken when it is wet and it is possible to make very neat fly bodies with it.

Marabou floss   A thicker floss but when cut into short lengths the strands can be untwisted and they will dress a range of sizes. I use the short lengths a lot for salmon fly tags.

Chenille   A popular body material, full bodied lures and flies can be tied with ease. Lay it on top of hookshank and tie in; wind it up to hookshank in close turns to make a fluffy full body. The bushier chenille can be used for large lures bodies and muddler minnow type heads. Speckled and fine chenille gives a very realistic nymph or fly body when tied in.

Raffia   Natural or plastic can be used as a body material. It creates a natural-looking fly body, is useful for detached mayfly bodies, and making shiny backs to beetle and fish fly dressings.

D.F.M.   Daylight Fluorescent Material, known as D.F.M., is available in white, grey, yellow, green, orange, scarlet, pink and blue. All these colours can be had in wool, floss and chenille but I would suggest, to start, acquiring the D.F.M. wool in only yellow, green and orange. It can be used for bodies, tags on lures and cheeks. D.F.M. wool can be chopped up and blended with furs and other materials to make a range of dubbings for all conditions.

Many synthetic materials are being offered in place of natural fur and hair and all have their place in fly-tying. However, I prefer the natural fur and hair of tradition which have stood the test of time, and hopefully will be used as long as the order of nature will allow.

Fur and hair   A wide range of animal furs are used as a dubbing medium to dress fly bodies. The most important to the tyer are seal's fur dyed a range of colours, hare's ear, mole fur and rabbit. Deer hair is most commonly used for spinning muddler minnow heads and clipped bodies for floating flies. The hair is a natural grey brown colour and it is surprising how the different types of deer hair vary in application.

There are a great variety of animals' tails available to the fly-tyer for tying hairwings. The most popular are grey squirrel, bucktail and calf tails dyed a wide range of colours. The tremendous range of bird wings and plumage available to the tyer are impossible to list here; later I list the game and exotic birds' feathers used in my dressings and describe the birds they came from.

Tinsel   I prefer the flat Lurex tinsel which is easy to work with and is ideal for tinsel bodies flies; softer than other tinsels, it does not tarnish and providing you rib it with oval tinsel or wire, it makes very neat tough durable bodies. It is available in gold and silver on spools and copper, gold and silver in flat sheets which can be cut to any width required. Superb flat embossed tinsel which gives a little more flash to fly bodies is used mainly for salmon flies – useful for ribbing longshank or treble or salmon tube flies; it is available in fine, medium or wide. Oval tinsel is primarily a ribbing tinsel for fly bodies or making tags on salmon flies and is available in a wide range of sizes.

Fly head varnish   There are various types and colours available and it is important that the fly head is properly finished off, otherwise the fly will fall apart. When tying hairwings or deer hair bodies always use enough varnish or cement dope to ensure durability to the dressing.

The most widely used feathers in fly-dressing come from the domestic chicken. The neck hackles from cocks and hens are used for dry and wet flies; the large saddle hackles are normally suitable for lure wings, and the small saddles can be used for palmer dressed flies. The spade hackle comes from the cocks' rump; the fibres can be used for dry fly tail whisks. Hackles are mainly available on the skin in cape form and buying feathers this way makes for easy hackle size selection for flies. Good quality dry fly capes are expensive especially in the rare colours. Hen capes are usually available in most colours without too much difficulty although the blues and duns are very scarce; however the colours for wet flies can be substituted by using coot, moorhen, partridge, wood pigeon, heron, and woodcock hackles.

For dry flies one of the difficulties for the embryo tyer is to know, when copying a pattern out of a book, what the various hackle colours are in relation to their name. Therefore I am listing the various hackle names and the range of colours they apply to:

Plain Colours

Cream   Ranges from off-white to very pale ginger; the quality is usually good. I like the yellowish capes for dyeing hot orange or yellow.

Red   Covers a very wide range of colour from very dark ginger to dark red. The reserve side of red hackles are very often lighter in colour. Capes with a very chalky reverse colour I normally dye black – they are not suitable for normal dry flies. The quality of the reds are on the whole superb.

White   The pure white capes are usually poor quality and the hackle shape varies tremendously; normally dyed various colours for general use.

Ginger   Pale ginger to dark ginger, hackles of this colour are usually of superb quality with a good shape. Some of the gingers have a darker colour in the centre of the hackle than on the outside. The dark ginger is a brownish colour with a suspicion of a black list; it is probably one of the most widely used colours in fly-dressing.

Jet black   A very rare colour in Old English game fowl. I have only ever seen two cocks of this colour and handled only a dozen capes in the last thirty years. Jet black hackles have a purple-green sheen which reflects when twisted in the light; it is a most beautiful hackle. The quality is usually adequate with a good reverse colour.

Black   Natural black is nowhere as black as a dyed hackle and the colour on the reverse side of the natural hackle is inclined to the dull. Black is not a pure colour, there are flecks of other colours in its make-up. Quality as a rule is poor.

Blue dun   The blues can be divided into three main groups; pale blue dun, medium blue dun and dark blue dun. Pale blue dun colour will range from almost blue-white up the colour of a herring gulls' back. Medium blue is from a sea gulls' back, to the shoulder plumage of a wood pigeon. Dark blue is from a pigeon shoulder plumage, up to the iron blue colour of a coots' shoulder.

As you can see there is quite a range of plain colours, so a dressing which lists blue dun as the hackle colour and no other details gives you quite a choice. There is also the difficulty of knowing where one colour or shade leaves off and the other one starts. It narrows down really to the tyer's choice. I don't think the fish are that fussy if the colour is near enough, considering that in many species the colour variation is quite remarkable, particularly in the insect and aquatic life forms. Therefore exact colouring is not that important; correct presentation is far more essential.

Barred, bi-colour or rare colours

Blood red   Very rare and a difficult colour to describe: it is rather like the colour of dried blood or a very dark mahogany; quality usually very good.

Badger   Colour will range from a white hackle to a yellow cream with a black list – quality variable, shape sometimes poor.

Golden or yellow badger   Covers a wide range of shades from light gold up to dark yellow, all with a black or near black list. Can be classified into three main groupings; light, medium and dark; shape and quality variable.

Furnace   A red hackle with black list ranging from dark ginger to dark red. Can be classified into three main groupings: light, medium and dark. The reverse colour is sometimes chalky or dull. Quality and shape usually adequate.

Coch-y-bondhu   A rare colour in the male bird. It is a dark ginger to dark red hackle with black list and edged with black. If a pattern dressing gives coch-y-bondhu it will be quite in order to use a furnace hackle in the correct shade – the fish will not notice.

Honey dun   Colour ranges from pale honey to dark golden honey with a blue list, which varies from light to dark according to the outside colouring of the hackle. Again there are three main groupings which can be classified into three shades; light honey dun, medium honey dun and dark golden honey dun. Quality and hackle shape variable.

Rusty dun   A blue hackle in the whole effect, speckled with rusty or golden flecks which can vary from small specks to large splashes or spots. There are three groupings; pale, medium and dark. Some dressings give a hackle name as brassy dun; this is a dun hackle which when held up to the light and twisted will give a golden or brassy sheen as it catches the light. It is usually a very speckled hackle.

Grizzle   Sometimes known as 'cuckoo'. A black and white barred hackle. Usually comes from a barred Plymouth Rock fowl.

Cree   A light ginger to dark ginger, with white or grey white bars. A very useful colour. Ideal hackle for dressing spent on mayflies, and winging crane flies. Quality usually adequate, sometimes very good.

Creole   This is a rare colour in Old English Game fowl. It is a barred hackle with the base colour white, or white grey barred with dark red bars. Never having seen a Creole bird or cape, I would think the quality and shape would be the same as any Old English Game.

Barred blue dun   One of my favourite colours, but it is very scarce. I produced my own by breeding a barred Plymouth cock to Old English Game Blue hen. There are a wide range of shades; the basic colour should be blue-white base with dark bars, whose colour stops well before positive black. In birds of my breeding the quality, colour and shape are superb.

There are a vast range of hackle colours; many so rare that it is not possible to classify them. The colours of some capes are so beautiful that they defy description; so rare and original, it is probable they are the only one of their type. I had a very fine yellow cream cape with every hackle on it edged with black, the only one I have ever seen like it.

For these fancy capes there are no names. However if you should acquire one with well-shaped stiff springy hackles, hang on to it. Providing the colour is near to whatever colour the pattern demands, it will not make any difference to the fish, and you will be using quality flies that float well. This in turn will improve your presentation, and hopefully add a sparkle to a day's fishing you will not easily forget.

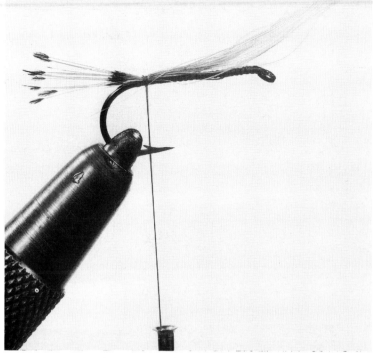

Plate 1: Mallard and Claret (page 71)

(*above*) Tying in golden pheasant tippets to form the tail.
(*below, left*) Rib already tied in, dubbing claret seal's fur on tying silk.
(*below right*) Dubbed body and rib completed. Secure rib and cut off.

Plate 2: Mallard and Claret continued

(*above*) Tying in the hackle.
(*left*) Winding the hackle.

Plate 3: Mallard and Claret continued

(*left*) Hackle wound and swept back ready for wing.
(*below*) Wing prepared and being judged for size.

Plate 4: Mallard and Claret continued

(*above*) Tying in the wing.
(*below*) Wing trimmed, head formed and whip finished. All that is needed now is a couple of
coats of varnish to complete the fly.

Plate 5: Black Streamer (page 81)

(*top*) Tying in black cock hackle fibres to form the tail.
(*centre*) Gold rib and black wool body tied in.
(*bottom*) Wool body wound and ribbed with gold oval tinsel.

*Plate 6: Black Streamer
continued*

(*Top*) Hackle tied in.
(*centre*) Hackle wound and
swept back ready for the wing.
(*bottom*) Four cock hackles
being judged for length to
form the wing.

Plate 7: Black Streamer continued

(*above*) Cock hackles prepared for tying in.
(*below*) Hackle wing tied in ready for doubling back.

Plate 8: Black Streamer continued

(*above*) Hackle wing doubled back and overtied.
(*below*) Wing and head tied to complete streamer. Now give head two coats of varnish.

2

Dressing the flies

Artificial flies can be divided into two groups: wet flies and dry flies. These groups can be divided again into sub-sections as hackled, winged, full feathered winged, hairwings, fully dressed, tubes and hackled winged flies.

I will endeavour to describe as clearly as possible the methods of dressing the various fly types. Fly-tying can be learned by the written word but a couple of hours instruction by a competent tyer is far more effective. It should be noted that there are no hard and fast rules in fly-tying and the methods I describe are my own; other tyers may do it differently. Do not despair if your first attempts look nothing like the flies in the book; with practise you will improve, we all had to start somewhere. I remember I tied my first flies using a pair of mole-grips balanced on a stack of books; the end result was terribly scruffy but effective.

Various furs, herls and quills are used for body materials in many patterns. To use or prepare for dressing they require special techniques.

Dubbed bodies To form a body of fur or wool first make sure the silk is well waxed (there is a liquid wax which can be used which is useful providing it is used sparingly). I find the pre-waxed silks and nylon threads are adequate. The art of successful dubbing is a waxed silk, small pinches of fur dubbed one at a time and moist fingertips.

To apply the dubbing, wet your fingertips and select a pinch of dubbing. Damp fingertips will help to hold the fur together (particularly seals' fur) when it is placed on the tying silk and they aid the rolling on of the dubbing. Take a pinch of fur between finger and thumb, hold the silk taut with the other hand, place fur on silk and roll it in one direction thus wrapping it around the tying silk. After completion of forward roll, open finger and thumb: the dubbing should now be in place.

Do not roll the dubbing forward and back as all that will accomplish is dubbing the fur on with the forward roll and then promptly taking it off on the reverse roll. Always roll the dubbing on in one direction. Repeat this until there is enough dubbing on the silk to form the fur body. Wind this body, or rather the dubbed silk, up the hookshank and then add the ribbing to complete the body.

Herls This is the term given to strands of feather fibres taken from the wing or tail quills and shoulder feathers of the larger birds. These feather strands are in fact lengths of quill with very short fibres or flue on them. To tie a herl body first select your herl and tie it in so that when the herl is wound, these short fibres stand at right-angles to the body, thus giving it a translucency which makes the pattern effective.

Quills The supply of quills is unlimited. They can be obtained from any quill come from the peacock's eye feather. When the flue is stripped the quills in the 'eye' have a double colour, brown and grey. When the quill is wound on the hookshank it gives a very realistic imitation of many insects. A quill so stripped can be dyed or coloured with felt pen. To strip 'eye' feather quills is not difficult but they are rather delicate and unless treated carefully are easily broken. To strip the quill I hold it by the root between finger and thumb, place it on a piece of glass and strip both sides of the quill with a dull razor blade. It is possible to remove the flue with hair removing cream and I have had variable success with this method. I found after covering the quill with cream, if you put too much on and have to wait longer for it to dry, the whole lot will just disintegrate. The secret I am sure is to lightly coat the quill with the cream and as soon as it is dry, brush it off with the flue.

Dry Fly – *Barred Blue Upright*
Materials required to tie this simple but effective pattern:
Hook   Size 14 wide gape
Tail   Whisks from barred blue dun spade hackle
Body   Stripped brown quill from peacock eye feather
Hackle   Barred blue dun cock hackle

The Barred Blue Upright is a variation I devised of R. S. Austin's famous Blue Upright and it has proved to be just as effective. If it is not possible to acquire a barred blue hackle, use instead a dark hackle from a barred Plymouth Rock cock.

1   Assuming the hook is in the vice, start winding the silk from the eye. To tie in the silk hold the loose end along the hookshank and wind from eye to hookshank thus trapping the end under turns of silk.

2   For the tail take three whisks from a spade hackle, taking advantage of any natural curving in the fibres. Tie in on the top of hookshank. Wind the silk up to the eye binding to the shank the loose ends of the tail whisks, then wind the silk back to the hook bend.

3   Tie the stripped quill at the tail with a couple of turns of silk and then wind the silk up to the hook eye. Before winding the quill, lightly coat the hookshank with varnish, then wind the quill to the hook eye leaving enough room to tie in the hackle. Lightly varnishing the hookshank before winding the quill will make the dressing much more durable.

4   Prepare the hackle for tying in. First strip off all the webbed and fluffy fibres. Run finger and thumb down the hackle, brushing the barbs nearly to right angles to the hackle stalk. Tie hackle in by the stripped butt on top of the hook making sure there is enough room to wind the hackle. The hackle must tie in so that the outside or weatherside of it is facing out over the hook eye, so that when it is wound the barbs are standing out at right angles. Take the tip of the hackle in the hackle pliers and take three or four turns with the hackle around the hookshank. The turns should almost touch but not overlap. After the turns are completed allow the hackle pliers to hang below the hook, still firmly attached to the hackle. Secure the hackle with a couple of turns of silk and then cut off the surplus hackle. Wind the silk carefully back through the wound hackle thus giving the fly more durability. Now complete a neat silk head, whip finish and varnish.

Palmer Hackled Wet Fly – *Yellow Sally*
Materials required:
Hook Size 12 wide gape
Body Seal's fur dyed yellow dubbed
Body hackle White hen hackle
Rib Gold Wire
Throat hackle Grey partridge hackle dyed yellow

A palmer fly is a fly with a hackle wound the length of its body. One of my most effective patterns is my dressing of the Yellow Sally which is very useful on both lake and river.

1 To tie the Yellow Sally wind silk to bend of the hook, tie in gold wire for ribbing. No tail is required. Dub the dyed yellow seal's fur on silk. Prepare body hackle and tie in at the shoulder and wind down body to bend of hook; allow hackle pliers to hang down, holding the hackle in position; now carefully wind the gold wire up the body binding down the hackle stem, taking care not to bind down any of the barbs. Secure the wire at the shoulder and cut off surplus.

2 Prepare partridge hackle to tie in at the throat, wind hackle. Complete head and whip finish.

Winging For quill feather wings the feather slips are taken one each from a left and right hand wing quill, placed together and tied in. Winging probably gives the beginner more difficulty than any other tying operation. The procedure for winging a standard wet fly is as follows: take feather slips from left and right hand quills, place on top of hook and check the length is correct. Pass the silk up between the thumb and nearside of wing and down between the finger and farside of wing. It is important at this stage that a loop of silk has been allowed to form above the wings. Draw this loop down firmly between finger and thumb so that the feather slips fibres come down one on top of the other. Keep gripping the wing firmly and repeat the loop over the top at least three times. Slide the fingers and thumb back so that the silk turns can be seen. Still holding the wing lay on a couple more turns of silk and then trim off surplus wing fibres and form a neat head, whip finish and varnish.

  For quill feather slips winging the following points should always be practised:
1 Make sure the silk foundation for wing is level.
2 Grip the wing firmly and always use the loop over the wing technique.
3 Do not let go of wings until three turns of silk have been looped over and drawn down.
4 If the wings split, take them off and start again.
5 Don't pull the silk after the wing has been released; when trimming surplus feather fibres or completing the head always hold the wings.

Winged Wet Fly – *Coachman*
Materials required:
Hook Size 8 wide gape
Body Three strands of peacock herl
Hackle Natural red cock
Wing White duck

1   To dress the Coachman, wind the silk from hook eye to hook band, tie in the three strands of peacock herl at hook bend, twist the peacock herl around the tying silk making a silk and peacock herl rope. Wind the silk and herl rope up the hookshank to form the body.

2   Prepare a medium red natural cock hackle and tie in. After winding the hackle sweep the barbs back so as to veil the body and overtie, thereby making a level bed for the wings.

3   Take the feather slips from a right and left hand white duck quill. Place them together and tie in thus forming the wings.

Whip finish knot   The finishing-off of a fly is most important and the whip finish technique in my view is the best. To apply the whip finish after completing the fly head, first make a loop. The loop should be made so that it is hanging below the fly and the bobbin holder end is laid against the hookshank looking back to the bend. Take the bottom of the loop and twist it so that it traps the bobbin holder end against the hookshank where the head of the fly is. Do this three times keeping firm pressure on the loop. Place point of scissors or dubbing needle in the loop making sure the tension is not relaxed. Catch hold of the bobbin and pull the loop closed, still keeping the pressure on to avoid the silk turns from slipping. When the loop has pulled the dubbing needle close to the head, slip it out and pull loop through the three turns of silk. The whip finish knot is now complete: after varnishing the fly it should never unwind and this is the difference between a quality fly and the other types.

The basic tying technique has now been covered and this should give the novice some knowledge of fly-tying. The following tips and techniques are intended to help the tyer with the more unusual aspects of the craft.

Glass beads for eyes   My method is to tie in glass beads into fly patterns to simulate eyes of various underwater creatures. First tie your fly in the normal manner, taking care to make the head a little longer than usual. Now take two beads and a short piece of nylon monofilament (the size of the beads and the breaking strain of the nylon are the tyer's choice – depending on the size of the fly or lure being tied). Thread the beads onto the nylon line and tie in the nylon close to hook eye with the beads on a loop lying over the fly body. Firmly pull the loose ends of the nylon until the beads are sitting snugly on the hookshank between the hackle and hook eye. Press down on the beads with your thumb until they are lying each side of the hookshank and then double the nylon line back so that it is lying on the fly body. Making sure that the nylon has passed between the beads on top of the hookshank, secure it with a few turns of silk. Now slowly pull the nylon line ends towards the hook bend and at the same time press down on the beads with the thumb; this will force the beads even further onto the sides of the hookshank. Keeping pressure on the nylon line so that it does not slip back, take a few more turns of silk between the beads and hackle, then secure the beads with figure of eight turns of silk. Cut off surplus nylon and whip finish. Now varnish liberally thus ensuring that the head and eyes are virtually indestructible. The technique will probably add only a minute or so to the time the average tyer takes to tie a fly. If you wish to impart additional life to the fly, tie peacock or ostrich herl between the hackle and beads which, when wound, give a bulky head. The use of beads sometimes makes flies more effective and there are virtually no wet fly patterns where they cannot be incorporated. It is, after all, the tyer's choice.

Tandem two hook mounts Place what is going to be the rear hook in the vice. Prepare a bed of silk down the hookshank. Take a piece of nylon monofilament of ten pound's breaking strain, lay it onto a hookshank and whip it on from eye to bend, bending the nylon back so that it is on top of the hookshank again and whip back to the hook eye and secure. You will now have a hook with a piece of nylon at least four inches long sticking out over the hook eye. Varnish the whipping and leave it dry. It is a good idea to prepare a dozen rear hooks at a time. When the varnish is dry, complete the body dressing of the rear hook for the tandem mount. Place the front hook of tandem mount in the vice, whip on a bed of silk, take the completed rear hook and lay the nylon line which is already tied into rear hook on the hookshank. Secure with a few turns of silk. Now check the distances between the rear and front hooks, making sure the gap is not too wide so that when the lure is completed and in use the rear hook cannot catch up in the front hook. Satisfied the distance is right, complete whipping on the nylon line from bend to eye. Doubling the nylon line back, whip down back to the hook bend, cut off the surplus nylon line and whip the silk back to the eye and whip finish. Varnish whipping. When varnish is dry complete the two hook tandem lure in the normal manner.

The same principle applies when tying flies with the flying treble hook. Instead of putting a body on the flying treble I always use a bright red, orange or yellow silk for the whipping and just varnish it; sometimes I will use gold or silver tinsel on the treble hook to give the fly a bit of flash. A tandem lure so constructed which is within the breaking strain of the double nylon line used is indestructible.

Butcher Tandem Lure
Materials required:
Hook Two size 6 wide gape
Tail Red wool
Body Silver tinsel, ribbed oval tinsel
Hackle Long fibred dyed red cock
Wing Black squirrel tail

Assuming the rear hook of mount is now ready to have the body dressed, wind the silk down the shank and tie in red wool tail at the bend of the hook. Wind the silk back up the hookshank, binding the wool down in even turns. Tie in oval tinsel at the eye and lay it on top of the hookshank, take the silk down to the bend of the hook, binding the oval tinsel down with even turns and return the silk to the eye Tie in the silver tinsel near the eye and take down the body with slightly open turns, checking to make sure that there is a neat turn by the wool tag then wind back up the body with the turns just touching. Bring the oval tinsel rib up in even spaced turns, tie in and cut off surplus. Complete the rear hook head, whip finish and varnish. When dry join it to the front hook as already described. Complete the body as above except there is no wool tag for the front hook. Take a long fibred dyed bright red cock hackle and tie in. Sweep this hackle back so that it veils the body. Cut enough black hair from squirrel tail to form the wing. Tie this hair as you would tie feather slips, with the loop over the top technique. Cut off surplus hair diagonally and varnish the hair tips liberally, complete head and whip finish and varnish liberally again. Secure for twenty-four hours and then varnish head with black varnish.

Dyeing   The material supplier can usually supply the fly-tyer with ready dyed furs and feathers. However there are, I know, many tyers who like to do the whole job themselves. The only utensils needed are an old saucepan and a small biscuit tin perforated like a colander which will stand inside the saucepan. It is a good idea to fashion a wire handle to the biscuit tin so that it can be easily lifted out of the saucepan when in use. The object of having a container that will drain freely is that it can be lifted out of the dye bath so that the dyeing process can be controlled. The only problem you may have using a tin as a colander is it may go rusty; if this happens, change the tin or acquire an aluminium container which is perforated. When preparing fur or feathers for dyeing, ensure that a highly concentrated detergent is used for washing the materials. If the grease or oil is not removed from items to be dyed, the results will not be very satisfactory. After washing, rinse the materials thoroughly and be sure there is no trace of detergent left. Fill the saucepan with hot water leaving enough spare room for the displacement of the water by the colander. Stand the saucepan over a gentle heat and add the dye; with experimenting you soon know how much to add. Place the materials into the colander and lower into the dye bath; after a couple of minutes remove the colander, add a tablespoon full of vinegar and stir to fix the colour and replace the colander in the mixture. To inspect the results lift the colander out of the dye and let it drain but remember the material will dry to a lighter shade than the one it is just after coming out of the dye bath.

When dyeing black always use dark coloured items such as dark red calf tails with no white hairs in their makeup; natural red poultry capes as a rule dye black fairly well but it may be necessary to leave the items in the dye for a couple of hours. The dye bath temperature should be maintained as high as possible without boiling. It may be necessary to add more water and dye because of evaporation.

Once the correct colour has been obtained, remove the items from the dye bath and rinse them out in cold water to remove any surplus dye. Place the materials between paper and press the water out of them, then shake the materials about and leave to dry. A very useful aid for colouring feathers, particularly deer hair which is not easy to dye unless it is white, is the felt tip waterproof marking pen. I use the felt pen a lot to colour the deer hair bodies of my sedge flies. It is possible to colour virtually any feather from stripped peacock quills to light coloured hackles in which you add all the bars or lists to whatever colour you fancy. I once tied up a series of hackled wet flies with a cream hackle marked with felt pen to give them a bright red list, and they were quite effective.

3

Fishing the Dry Fly and the Dry Flies of Old

Fishing the dry fly can be practised from the bank or boat on river or lake; there are a wide range of insects which hatch, lay eggs or just get blown onto the water to be eaten by trout; it is up to the angler to take advantage of natural occurrences and present to the fish an artificial fly dressing as near as possible to the natural; if this is done correctly the end result may be the memory of a lifetime.

When fishing still waters, particularly the large reservoirs, trout will be seen moving to the water surface taking flies or nymphs, and to discover exactly what they are feeding on may not be easy. It could be they are taking flies like sedges, etc. On the other hand pupae may be coming to the surface prior to hatching. Sit for a while and watch the water; as the angler becomes more experienced in lake fishing it is possible for him to tell the difference in the rise forms of the fish. He will not always get it right, but it makes for interesting fishing.

When there is a reasonable wind blowing across the lake, wind-slicks will form. In these slicks which consist of flat water cutting a strip through a ripple like a knife, food items will collect. Very often you will observe a fish travelling upwind in this slick, rising here or there taking food in the windlane, probably a sedge dropped in front of it at the right time will provoke a rise. The best dry fly fishing on lakes during the day depends a great deal on suitable weather conditions. Usually the ideal day is warm with a gentle breeze which provides a useful ripple on the lake's surface. A good cloud cover gives perfect conditions, especially if there are a few sedge flies flittering on the water. Very bright cloudless hot days with little or no wind will prove to be difficult for any type of fly fishing on lakes, particularly in a flat calm. On cold wet windy days, especially early in the season, don't bother with the dry fly, stick to lures and wet flies.

Observation of any movement on the surface is very important. Often it is possible to tell in which direction fish are travelling if they are nose and tailing or if the actual rise has been observed. A useful tactic is to cast the fly out to the point where you think the fish will pass and wait for it to arrive. Very often the sudden rise to the fly will give you a start; it appears as the fish has come from nowhere. Lift the rod tip and tighten – usually fish that have taken the fly like this are well hooked. This method is not so easy during a widespread general rise. I usually cast the fly out and wait for it to be taken or if a fish moves close I will cover it; sometimes it is just guesswork in what direction the fish has taken. If I get it right at least half the time in these wide spread rises I am reasonably satisfied. Also remember trout, when on the surface, normally always move up-wind.

Fishing the dry fly on rivers is basically the same as lakes except the rising fish usually take surface food on station. As the river flows over its bed, these fish lie in their feeding stations ready to intercept any food items that may come over them in the flow. They will move off station to take flies which pass within their window; however at times they can become very selective.

The angler can make use of the river flow to present his fly but care must be taken to make sure drag does not take place causing the fly to skate across the surface. The cause of drag is the fly-line being caught in the waterflow, thus forming a belly in the line downstream of the angler, which in turn speeds the fly up so that it skates across the surface, putting fish down. It is possible to reduce the risk of drag by casting the fly and at the same time forming a line belly upstream but the flow of the water will soon reverse the situation. If it has been done properly it will allow enough travel on the water for the fly to pass over the fish correctly. Before the drag sets in, if the fish has not taken, lift off and cast again. On the swift-flowing Cornish rivers if there is no obvious rise it pays to fish the water. Cast the dry fly into any run or eddy; let it drift into the bankside under any overhanging vegetation. Where there are rocks sticking up or just below the surface in the river, cast upstream of them and let the flow of the river fish the fly around for you. Very often good size trout can lie in these places and trout in these rocky rain-fed rivers are free risers. They can take and eject a fly quicker than it takes to blink, more fish are missed than hooked.

When fishing the dry fly it is essential they float well. The artificial of the upwinged flies needs to be dressed with a good stiff cock hackle free of web from a matured cock to give the artificial a lightness equal to the natural insect. For fast or rough waters the palmer hackle dressing will probably be the more suitable. The stoneflies and sedges can be more heavily dressed. I prefer deer hair for dressing the bodies on these imitations which after waterproofing makes the fly virtually unsinkable. There are plenty of floatants available to waterproof the dry flies but use this aid sparingly and take care you do not get any on your leader. After catching a trout on the dry fly it will be necessary to wash it clean of fish slime and blood and before waterproofing make sure it is absolutely dry. I normally change to another fly of the same pattern, sticking the used one in my hat to dry; when it is dry I waterproof it ready to go again.

It would appear that James Ogden of Cheltenham was the first to describe how to dress the dry fly in his little book published in 1879, _Ogden on Fly Tying_, where he claimed to be the orginator of Floating Flies, having introduced them to his clients some forty years earlier.

A contender for the honour of tying the first dry fly was David Foster who was associated with the tackle firm, Foster of Ashbourne. If James Ogden was accurate with the dating of his introduction of the dry fly, and there is no evidence to suggest otherwise, it would appear that he predated David Foster by at least ten years. The bi-centenary booklet issued by the firm of Fosters in the early 1960s lists the winged dry fly as tied by David Foster in 1854. As all this happened over 130-odd years ago, any conclusion on my part would be pure conjecture. It is, I suppose, possible that Foster and Ogden were known to each other and discussed fishing and fly dressing.

There is no doubt they lived in an age which saw a rapid change in fly-dressing methods and the improved techniques of fishing the artificial fly. Around this time the eyed fishing hook was introduced; prior to this the hooks were attached to gut which wore out or just got brittle and broke off. Ogden's method of tying the dry fly is interesting: he dressed his flies with the wing in the upright position and split rather like the modern dressing. The wings were prepared in the same manner as today, taking matching feather slips from right and left handed quills, placing together and tying in. Ogden's instructions for this method in his book appears to have been the first time it has been described in print. (The normal winging technique at that time was a single strip of feather which was doubled and then tied in; this wing was split into two halves with figure of eight turns of silk to simulate the wings of the insect.)

Ogden was a professional fly-tyer and was dependent on the goodwill of the angling public for his living and would dress whatever flies the client required. However for his own patterns he was careful to match the colour of the artificial as near as possible to the natural insect. He tells of visits to the river catching specimens and examining them with a magnifying glass so as to be able not only to match the colour but also the correct size of the natural. Two dressings devised by Ogden which have survived the test of time and have been used by generations of fly-fishers, are the Hare's Ear or Lug, and that versatile fly, 'The Invicta'.

The year 1879 saw another major development of the dry fly, when George Selwyn Marryat met Frederic Maurice Halford (who was destined to become guru of the dry-fly cult) in a tackle shop in Winchester. Halford in discussion with Marryat let it be known that he was having problems with fly-tying; this chance remark proved to be the stepping-stone to the writing of Halford's book, *Floating Flies and How to Dress Them*.

In the early part of the following year Halford made his headquarters on the river Test near Houghton Mill. Here, with Marryat, he began to study riverside insects, the materials to dress them and to develop the necessary tying skills to be able to reproduce them in fur and feather. It was not until six years later that the results of their collaboration was published. Halford suggested that *Floating Flies and How to Dress Them* should be published under their joint names, but Marryat for reasons known only to himself, declined. There can however be no doubt that but for Marryat's collaboration this book would never have materialised.

As time went by Halford was to become more involved in the dry fly, always searching for the exact representation to such an extent that he attracted a following of disciples who held such extreme purist views that anybody who fished wet flies or nymphs were abused or held up to ridicule. Marryat was not drawn into this argument and was quite content to make the point that if conditions were such that it was impossible to fish the dry fly, he had no objections to fishing it wet. This is, in my view, an assessment by a realistic mature fly fisherman. Marryat died in 1896 and was buried at Winchester; perhaps it was a blessing he was never to know Halford in his high priest role when he became contemptuous of any fly fishing method other than the dry fly – I am sure Marryat would not have approved. Unfortunately the extreme purist attitude was carried on by Halford's followers for many years after his death in 1914 and there are some waters I believe that are still reserved exclusively for the dry fly.

In the list of dry fly dressings below, I give some of the patterns from the tyers of the past which are still as effective as the day they were created. The tyings are given as the old masters intended and any variation of dressing because the materials are not available are listed after the pattern. The hook sizes are to the Redditch Scale.

Patterns of James Ogden, 1879

Red Spinner
Hook　Size 10, 12, 14, 16 wide gape
Body　Ruddy brown floss
Ribbing　Fine gold twist
Wings　Dark starling, broad and upright
Hackle　Dark red cock
Whisks　Dark red cock hackle fibres dressed long

The Hare's Ear
Hook　Size 14, 12, 10 wide gape
Body　Hare's ear or face. Spun on yellow silk
Tag　Fine gold tinsel
Wings　Starling, set full and very upright
Hackle　Dubbing picked out
Whisks　Red cock hackle fibres

Ogden says for a change use a body of yellow silk only and hare's ear hacklewise for the legs. For variety, use hare ear body with fine gold tinsel or twist, and wing with woodcock. I would omit the starling wings and tie in a medium shade red cock hackle in place of the picked out dubbing for legs; this would virtually give the modern tie for the Hare's Ear.

Alder
Hook　Size 12, 10 wide gape
Tag　Dark claret mohair
Body　Bronze peacock (with reddish brown tying silk) herl
Wing　Hen pheasant centre tail, full and long
Hackle　Dark brassy dun cock hackle, or black cock hackle

I would change the mohair for seal's fur and use a dark furnace cock hackle.

Oak Fly or Downlooker
Hook　Size 12, 10 wide gape
Silk　Lead coloured showing at the head and shoulders
Body　Bright orange floss
Hackle　Furnace cock palmer fashion snipped off at top
Wings　Woodcock dressed flat

Whirling Blue Dun
Hook　Size 12, 10 wide gape
Body　Reddish brown fur from squirrel legs, spun on yellow silk, waxed with white wax
Wings　Dark starling (upright)
Hackle　Pale ginger cock
Whisks　Three fibres red cock hackle

Patterns of George S. Marryat, 1880

Red Tag
Hook　Size 12, 10 wide gape
Tag　Ibis or scarlet wool
Body　A single strand of herl from the tail feather of a blue yellow macaw
Hackle　Blood red game cock

Needle Brown
Hook   Size 12 or 10 wide gape
Tag   Primrose floss silk
Body   Orange tying silk
Hackle   Honey dun cock

Patterns of Frederic M. Halford, 1886

Autumn Dun
Hook   Size 14 wide gape
Body   Natural heron herl
Wings   Snipe
Hackle   Pale blue dun cock
Whisks   Fibres from pale blue dun hackle

Hackle Blue Quill
Hook   Size 14 wide gape
Body   Natural brown peacock quill
Hackle   Pale honey dun cock
Whisks   Honey dun hackle fibres

Grizzly Blue
Hook   Size 14 wide gape
Body   Pale mole fur spun on pale yellow silk
Hackle   Grizzled blue cock

Yellow Bumble
Hook   Size 14 wide gape
Body   Primrose floss silk ribbed strand of peacock sword
Hackle   Pale blue dun cock

Orange Bumble
Hook   Size 14 wide gape
Body   Orange floss silk ribbed with strand of peacock sword and with flat gold tinsel
Hackle   Honey dun cock

The hook sizes I have given are intended only as a general guide; it is up to the tyer to decide what to use depending on the water he is fishing. Halford's patterns given are useful summer and autumn flies. The Orange Bumble is particularly effective on grayling.

The counties of Cornwall and Devon are renowned for their game fishing and are also noted for the quality of their fly-tyers. The most famous fly-tyer the two counties have ever produced was R. S. Austin of Tiverton. The reason for this was the creation of one fly, and it was this single dressing and the mystery of its body material which propelled its creator from obscurity into a secure niche in flytying history.

As a young man Austin saw action in the Crimean War, serving with the Royal Artillery. On leaving the army he settled in Tiverton where he set himself up as a tobacconist and professional fly-tyer. Towards the end of the nineteenth century, Austin was in regular correspondence with G. E. M. Skues, a well known authority on all matters concerning trout flies and their dressings. Sending Skues a new dressing he had devised, Austin explained that it had proved deadly and had taken trout which had proved difficult previously, some of them large fish by any standards. Skues returned the fly and enquired as to the nature of the dubbing; Austin sent a packet of dubbing with full details of the new fly.

Meanwhile Skues dressed a batch of flies as Austins's pattern and fished the fly on the river Wandle during the last few days of the 1900 season. The results he recorded amazed him as without changing his position he rose no fewer than eighteen trout, although he failed to hook many of them because overhead branches preventing him from tightening properly. The start of the 1901 season saw Skues on the banks of the river Itchen determined to give this un-named fly a comprehensive testing for the season. Covering only one hundred yards of bank he succeeded in taking seven brace of trout. A report of Skues' excellent day duly appeared in print and the fly's name was given as the Tups Indispensable. The resulting publicity this fly received kept Austin fully employed turning out Tups Indispensable by the hundreds if not thousands.

I am of the view that the mystery of the body material and the success of the dressing as a fish catcher created a fly that to anglers was infallible. For many years after the introduction of the Tups even up to today, there are all sorts of body colours sailing under the name of Tups Indispensable. For the experienced tyer to make up a dubbing mixture to a colour is reasonably simple providing there is a sample to work from; it may not be possible to recognise all the ingredients but it is not difficult to mix the colour correctly. I am rather surprised that there were not more tyers at that point in time able to copy the dressing correctly – so that it looked like the real thing.

I don't know what the Tups Indispensable was supposed to represent, some knowledgable writers have expressed various opinions but nobody is really sure. I am inclined to accept the view that Tups Indispensable, like the Gold Ribbed Hare's Ear, is effective throughout the season and it is a good general pattern representing no particular insect.

The well known patterns, the Blue Upright and Half Stone, along with the Tups Indispensable, are probably the only patterns of R. S. Austin that are still offered on the fly-seller's lists.

Patterns of R. S. Austin, 1890

Hook sizes range from 12 to 18.

Blue Upright
Body   Brown peacock's quill
Hackle   Dark blue cock (occasionally rusty)
Whisks   Dark blue cock
Tying silk   Cream

This fly is very useful throughout the season and I have devised two very effective variations of it which I shall be giving in my pattern list.

Red Fly
Body   Orange floss
Ribbing   Peacock herl from eye
Hackle   Red cock dressed palmer style
Tying silk   Brown

Very useful throughout the season; I have some really cracking days with it. It is really deadly when fished wet in fast runs or eddys when the trout are not coming to the surface fly.

Half Stone
Body   Bright yellow floss silk
Hackle   Dark blue cock
Whisks   Dark blue cock
Tying silk   Cream

Again another useful dressing which is very effective throughout the season. I have had such memorable days with it that I have devised a good variation that is fished wet or sub surface.

Honey Dun Half Stone
Body   Bright yellow floss
Hackle   Honey dun cock
Whisks   Honey dun cock
Tying silk   Cream

Useful throughout the season.

Dark Gold Twist
Body   Hare's flax from back of hare
Ribbing   Gold twist
Hackle   Medium blue cock
Whisks   Medium blue cock
Tying silk   Cream

Good pattern when March Browns are hatching.

Heron Blue Body
Body   Heron wing quill herls
Hackle   Medium blue cock
Whisks   Medium blue cock
Tying silk   Cream

Dark Blue Dun
Body   Water Rat fur dubbed
Tying silk   Yellow
Tag   Turn of gold tinsel
Hackle   Darkish blue cock
Whisks   Darkish blue cock

Badger
Body   Mulberry silk
Tag   Red tinsel
Hackle   Badger cock

Good for fishing runs and stickles when there is no apparent rise, also useful if fished wet.

Yellow Quill
Body   Pale watery yellow quill
Hackle   Medium blue cock
Tying silk   Cream

Yellow Dun
Body   Light coloured fur from hare dyed yellow
Ribbing   Fine gold twist
Hackle   Light blue cock
Whisks   Light blue cock
Tying silk   Yellow

Red Spinner (Tups Indispensable)
Body   White ram's testicle wool and lemon fur from spaniel in equal parts. Little hare's poll fur and red seal's fur to give pinkish tinge. (Do not overdress body.)
Hackle   Yellow spangled lightish blue cock
Whisks   Yellow spangled lightish blue cock

A good all round pattern throughout the season. I have dressed it with a yellow grizzle hackle and whisks and added enough red seal's fur to make the thorax red.

Jenny Spinner
Body   White horsehair
Tying silk   Crimson at head and tail
Hackle   Silvery blue cock
Whisks   Silvery blue cock
Useful from the end of April onwards.

Red Tag
Body   Peacock herl slightly dyed magenta
Tag   Red floss
Tying silk   Claret
Hackle   Furnace cock

This dressing is effective wet or dry. Dress the wet fly version with hen hackle. It is good when fished wet late in the evening. Effective throughout the season.

Pale Evening Dun
Body   Very light fawn opossum (use underbelly hare's fur)
Hackle   Lightish medium blue cock
Whisks   Lightish medium blue cock
Tying silk   Cream

Good throughout the summer to end of season; in warm weather and low water conditions will sometimes save the angler a blank day. Very good late evenings after hot summer's day.

Orange Drake (Spent Fly)
Body   Wool half orange, half brown
Hackle   Honey dun cock
Whisks   Honey dun cock
Wings   Light starling
Tying silk   Orange

Instead of wool I use seal's fur for the body, lightly dressed. If honey dun is not available for the hackle use a yellow badger or honey ginger.

Grey Quill Gnat
Body   Light peacock quill
Hackle   Two turns long fibred silver-blue cock
Wings   Light starling
Tying silk   Cream

This is not a complete list of R. S. Austin dry fly patterns; I have only listed what I know to be effective. If the hackle colours prove difficult to find, you can substitute the silvery blue for a light grizzle, honey dun for yellow badger and medium blue for grizzle.

4

Dry Flies of Today

Over the years I have devised a number of different dressings to represent the upwinged, sedges and stoneflies. The list of flies I have compiled are my most effective dressings; the upwinged patterns I have dressed in the main without wings, as I feel unless the wings are dressed spent or partly spent, there is no great advantage in having upright split wings. The hackle version will float and takes fish just as well as the winged dressing. On my sedge and stonefly dressings I like to use whole feathers for the wings. I dress these feathers flat on top of the body so that when viewed from below, the outline of the artificial looks like the real thing.

Barred Blue Upright
Tying silk   Grey
Body   Brown peacock quill
Hackle   Barred blue dun cock
Whisks   Barred blue dun cock
Hook   Size 14, 16, wide gape

Barred Yellow Upright
Tying silk   Naples yellow
Body   Brown peacock quill
Hackle   Yellow grizzle cock
Whisks   Yellow grizzle cock
Hook   14, 16, wide gape

The Barred Blue Dun and Barred Yellow Upright are two very effective variations of R. S. Austin's Blue Upright and over the years have taken a lot of trout. The two patterns are effective from late April until early August and then, from late August, evenings only when fish are moving.

Red Quill
Body   Peacock quill dyed red spinner
Wing   Grey mallard or teal
Hackle   Red cock
Whisks   Red cock

Ginger Quill
Body   Peacock quill dyed red spinner
Wing   Grey mallard or teal
Hackle   Ginger cock
Whisks   Ginger cock

Blue Winged Olive
Body   Peacock quill dyed medium olive
Wings   Pale coot
Hackle   Dyed medium olive cock
Whisks   Dyed medium olive cock

The Stonefly and Half Stone are variations of Austin's dressings but I consider them to be more effective. They seem to be a good general representation of the smaller stoneflies ranging from the Yellow Sally to the Needle Fly. They will very often rise fish when there is no surface activity. The hook size can range between size ten to size fourteen wide gape.

Half Stone
Tying silk　Yellow
Body　Dyed yellow goose herl
Hackle　Dark blue dun

Stonefly
Tying silk　Yellow
Tag　Four turns yellow silk or floss
Body　Dyed yellow goose herl
Body hackle　Grizzle cock
Hackle　Dark blue dun

Black Gnat
Tying silk　Grey
Body　Blue heron quill
Body hackle　Black cock
Hackle　Black cock
Whisks　Black cock
Hook　Size 14 wide gape

Red Ant
Tying silk　Mulberry
Body　Slips of cork shaped as ant body, covered with turns of silk then varnished.
Wing　Grey mallard
Hackle　Red Cock

Black Ant
Same as Red Ant except tying silk and hackle is black. Hook size 10, 12, 14, wide gape.

Very often in late April there is a big hatch of hawthorn flies which can bring the trout on to the boil. Some years this can occur in May and even in June if it has been a cold Spring.

Hawthorn Fly
Body　Black cock wound palmer fashion and clipped close to hookshank
Legs　Black goose herl extending beyond hook bend
Wing　Coot hackle tied flat
Hackle　Black cock

Red Sedge
Tail　Red cock hackle fibres
Body　Red cock hackle dressed palmer fashion
Wing　Brown partridge hackle tied flat
Hackle　Red cock
Hook　Size 10 mayfly

Grizzle Series *(Dry or Wet)*

Grizzle and Yellow
Tail　Grizzle cock fibres

Body　Yellow silk and palmer grizzle hackle for dry fly. Yellow seal's fur and gold oval tinsel for wet fly

Hackle   Grizzle cock
Hook   Size 8, 10, 12, 14, wide gape

Grizzle and Orange
Dressing as above, except orange silk for dry fly or orange seal's fur for wet fly.

Grizzle and Green
Dressing as above, except green silk for dry fly or grannon seal's fur for wet fly.

Grizzle and Red
Dressing as above, except red silk for dry fly or red seal's fur for wet fly.

Rough water floaters

I have designed the next range of sedge flies with deer hair as body material. The floating properties of deer hair are very well known, as flies so tied are virtually unsinkable; probably only cork bodied flies are better. To tie deer hair bodies start first by taking four or five turns of silk on the hookshank approximately in line with the hook barb below. If I am tying in a tail I will tie the feather fibres on top of these four or five turns of silk and then overtie, thus making a bright tag of whatever colour is required, at the same time leaving the remainder of hookshank bare for spinning the deer hair.

After coating the hookshank with varnish start spinning the deer hair on in small lots: taking a pinch of hair from the deer skin, lay it on the hookshank and very carefully wind two loose turns of silk around the hair and hookshank, keeping hold of the hair and making sure it is all in place. Gently take up the slack in the silk; if satisfied the hair is correctly in position release it, at the same time pulling taut the silk, thus causing the hair to flare out around the hookshank. Continue spinning pinches of deer hair with drops of varnish between each spinning until the hookshank is covered.

I usually tie up a half a dozen deer hair bodies at a time as by the time the last one is completed the first is dry enough to be clipped. Trim all the hair off the top and underneath of the hookshank until you are left with a flat wedge of deer hair. Trim the sides of the wedge carefully until you have a reasonable body shape – not a round body but a flatish shape more like the natural insect.

For the wing tie in a game-bird hackle carefully selected for colour and stripped to the right size. Tie it in flat near the hookeye, pulling the hackle stalk over the hookeye until the leading fibres of the hackle just start going under the silk; this will cause the hackle to lie flat on the deer-hair body and perhaps slightly envelope it. It is important that all the deer hair bodied flies have their wing tied in flat on top of the body; any other style will detract from the effectiveness of the design.

If required, tie in the horns and then the cock hackle which is wound as normal. On some dressings you can tie in two game-bird hackles flat on top of the deer hair and use their stalks as horns. Deer hair can be dyed – obviously for bright colours use white hair and for a speckled effect to the body, use a waterproof felt pen; they are available in virtually any colour. The waterproof marking pen is very useful for colouring a list on light coloured hackles. I have coloured cream hackles with a bright red list which, when tied into a fly, gives it a very attractive look.

Cinnamon Sedge (*Plate 9*)
Tying silk   Brown

Body   Natural deer hair spun and clipped, speckle marked with felt pen (green)

Wing   Two light woodcock hackles, stalks to be left to form the horns
Hackle   Light ginger cock
Hook   Size 14 mayfly

Hatches of this sedge are rather sparse; it usually appears in June and carries on right through the season. It is a very common species and extremely useful sedge fly for the fly fisherman.

Grouse Wing Sedge
Tying silk   Brown
Body   Natural deer hair spun and clipped, speckle marked with felt pen (brown)
Wing   Dark woodcock or grouse hackles
Hackles   Dark red furnace cock
Hook   Size 12 mayfly

These sedge flies are very common, appearing in June and lasting through until September; sometimes they can be seen in very large concentrations. They usually hatch out late afternoon or early evening.

Silverhorns can be observed most sunny days after June; usually they stay close to the bank in the shelter of any trees or bushes. I have seen them on a windy day sheltering in the rushes beside a lake. The adults are useful for taking trout, but when the silverhorns and longhorns are hatching on the water (which sometimes can be in very large swarms) the pupae are very eagerly sought after by the trout; fish the sedge artificial on the point with the pupae artificial on the dropper. This combination can be at times very effective, in fact deadly.

Black Silverhorn
Tying silk   Black
Body   Dyed black deer hair spun and clipped
Wing   Blue black pheasant hackle
Horns   Stalks of small grizzle hackles
Hackle   Black cock
Hook   Size 12 wide gape

Black Silverhorns are quite common and widely distributed and when seen in silhouette can be sometimes mistaken for the brown silverhorns. They appear in June, very often hatching out during the day.

Brown Silverhorn
Tying silk   Brown
Body   Natural deer hair spun and clipped, speckle marked with felt pen (green)
Wing   Woodcock hackle
Horns   Stalks of small grizzle hackles
Hackle   Dark ginger cock
Hook   Size 12 wide gape

Mottled Sedge (*Plate 9*)
Tying silk   Brown
Body   Natural deer hair spun and clipped, speckle marked with felt pen (green)
Wings   Reddish brown pheasant hackle edged with black, can be mottle marked with felt
   pen (brown). Stalks to be left to form the horns.
Hackle   Ginger cock
Hook   Size 12 mayfly

The mottled sedge is a fairly large fly, similar in size to the large cinnamon sedge. It is a handsome sedge fly and the wing colour does vary quite a bit from cream brown to pale yellow brown with brown patches, which give the mottled effect. They are usually observed from late May and can be still around in October; a useful fly right through the fishing season.

Caperer
Tying silk Orange
Body Natural deer hair spun and clipped and coloured all over with felt pen (orange)
Wing Reddish brown pheasant hackles. Stalks left for horns
Hackle Medium ginger cock
Hook Size 10 mayfly

One of the best known sedge flies due to the fact that William Lunn, celebrated river keeper and fly tyer of the river Test, devised an artificial by that name.

It is a common and widely distributed species and usually appears towards the end of August and stays around until October. Hatches are often sparse, usually commencing late afternoon or early evening; due to this the fly is continuously dancing or fluttering over the water – hence their name. The adults hatch out in open water and scuttle for the bank leaving a distinct vee-shaped wake. Due to their large size and the dancing on the water the trout will take them avidly.

Large Red Sedge (*Plate 9*)
Tying silk Claret
Body Natural deer spun and clipped, speckle marked with felt pen (brown)
Wing Two reddish brown pheasant hackles. Stalks to be left to form horns
Hackle Red cock
Hook Size 12 mayfly

Hatches are usually from mid May to July. They are fairly common although I have only seen the odd one at a time, mainly in the evenings. I have taken some good fish on the artificial even when there has been no natural fluttering about.

Brown Sedge
Tying silk Orange
Body Natural deer spun and clipped, speckle marked with felt pen (orange)
Wing Brown partridge hackles
Hackle Dark furnace cock
Hook Size 10 wide gape

A medium sized species, autumn hatching, which usually starts appearing in September. Shelters in the bankside vegetation. It is widely distributed and hatches out in considerable numbers. I have often walked through the rushes on the water's edge, forcing them to fly so that they drift out onto the water, thus provoking a rise.

Welshman's Button
Tying silk Black
Body Dyed brown deer hair spun and clipped
Hackle Red cock
Hook Size 10 or 12 wide gape

The name Welshman's Button is so well known there cannot be many flyfishers who have not heard of it. This name was given to the sedge fly by F. M. Halford and since that time it has generally been accepted. It is common on rivers but I have not seen many on lakes, however it is a useful fly and the dressing given will take fish on river or lake. The natural usually appears from June onwards.

Black Sedge
Tying silk Black
Body Dyed black deer hair spun and clipped
Wing Blue black pheasant hackle
Hackle Black cock
Hook Size 10 or 12 wide gape

An all-black insect slightly larger than the silverhorn although similar. They are widely distributed but mainly seen on the rivers; can be sometimes observed in little swarms flying close to the banks. They appear in May or June and last until about August, depending a little on the year.

Grey Sedge
Tying silk White
Body Natural deer hair spun and clipped
Wing Grey partridge
Hackle Badger cock
Hook 10, 12, 14, wide gape

A small fly which can be seen on both lakes and rivers quite widely distributed and is most common during summer. The above dressing can also be used to imitate the medium stonefly which usually appears in April, thus giving the dressing quite a long season.

Alder
Tying silk Red
Body Natural deer hair spun and clipped and coloured with felt pen (magenta)
Wing Woodcock hackle
Hackle Black cock
Hook Size 10 or 12 wide gape

A common and widely distributed fly, known as a very killing fly on the rivers despite the fact that F. M. Halford denounced it as valueless to fly fisherman. In recent years it has also been recognised as a useful lake fly, mainly in its larval form. Fishing the dry pattern with the wet version of the alder produces a combination on the lakes which takes fish on the surface and below. The adult appears in May and swarms mostly in the shelter of bushes and rushes in the vicinity of water and over water itself.

The Colliford Heather and Dung Flies are new designs I devised in 1985. In 1986 Chris Martindale and I gave them a thorough testing and they proved to be extremely effective when the natural fly was in season. Some of the brown trout Chris Martindale took on the Dung Fly dressing had taken the fly right back in their throats and it was impossible to unhook them without first killing the fish. These are two very effective new designs for Colliford Lake and there is no reason they should not be as effective elsewhere.

Colliford Heather Fly
Tying silk Red
Body Deer hair in three parts: black-red-black, spun and clipped
Wing Blue black pheasant

Hackle   Black cock
Hook   Size 10 or 12 wide gape

The heather fly, like the hawthorn fly, is a terrestrial. It is similar in size and appearance to the hawthorn, the only difference being the reddish colour on tops of legs and underbody. It sometimes appears in large numbers and when it is blown onto the water it is of considerable value to the fly-fisher as the trout will take the flies avidly. It is in season longer than the hawthorn, usually appearing in August and lasting to the end of the season. The dressing I devised for Colliford is particularly effective, even when there is only the odd natural about.

Colliford Dung Fly
Tying silk   Red
Body   Dyed bright yellow deer hair spun and clipped
Wing   Grey partridge
Hackle   Ginger cock
Hook   Size 12 wide gape

The dung flies appear in June although there will be some about earlier. A very important fly for the lake fisherman and my dressing is a particularly good floater.

Mayfly Dun
Tying silk   Brown
Body   Off-white deer hair spun and clipped
Hackle   Badger and olive cock wound together
Tail   Three fibres from cock pheasant centre tail
Hook   Size 12 or 10 mayfly

Mayfly Spinner
Tying silk   White
Body   Slips of cork overtied with white silk and varnished, ribbed with black silk
Hackle   Off-white deer hair spun and trimmed on top and underneath hookshank, thus
   leaving deer hair on sides of hookshank in spent position
Tail   Three fibres from cock pheasant centre tail
Hook   Size 10 or 12 mayfly

Large mayfly hatches in Cornwall are not a common event and only once have I witnessed a decent hatch taking place; this was on the river Inny, a tributary of the Tamar, about six years ago. However it pays to carry the artificial in your fly box; tiny hatches of mayfly do occur from time to time right up to the beginning of August.

Dapping Flies

On larger lakes, if the wind blows up a bit, you will have quite a heavy swell or a big wave getting up. If this should happen during the summer when the fish are in the top layers of water, this will give the angler a chance to use the dapping technique, which can give some exciting fishing. I have devised some very bushy flies for dapping and on the right day they can be very effective.

Grey Dapper
Tail   Grizzle cock hackle fibres
Body   Two grizzle hackles wound up hookshank

Hackle   Large badger cock hackle
Hook   Size 8 mayfly

Red Dapper
Tail   Cree cock hackle fibres
Body   Two dark cree hackles wound up hookshank
Hackle   Dark red furnace cock
Hook   Size 8 mayfly

White Dapper
Tail   Badger cock hackle fibres
Body   Two yellowish-cream hackles wound down hookshank
Hackle   Large badger cock
Hook   Size 8 mayfly

Dark Dapper
Tail   Dark red furnace cock hackle fibres
Body   Two black cock hackle wound down hookshank
Hackle   Dark red cock hackle
Hook   Size 8 mayfly

There are plenty of opportunities to dap on lakes on a windy day, particularly when the water has warmed up and the wind has pushed up a big wave. This is about the only chance for the angler fishing from the bank to use this technique. There will not be that many fish hooked in relation to the number of rises, but plenty of excitement with the splashy rises these dapping flies provoke.

Daddy-Longlegs No 1 *(Plate 9)*
Legs   Moose hair
Body   Peacock herl
Wings   Cree cock hackles
Hackle   Cree cock
Hook   Size 10 mayfly

Daddy-Longlegs No 2 *(Plate 9)*
Legs   Cock Pheasant centre tail fibres knotted
Body   Curved rubber band
Wings   Cree cock hackles
Hackle   Cree cock
Hook   Size 10 mayfly

Daddy-Longlegs No 3 *(Plate 9)*
Legs   Cock pheasant centre tail fibres knotted
Body   Deer hair clipped and coloured with felt pen (green)
Wings   Cree cock hackles
Hackle   Cree cock

In 1973 Arnold Curtis and I were sharing a boat at Crowdy Marsh Lake. Sport was slow, we had tried various tactics and caught the odd fish, but the fishing was very dour. Arnold rummaged through his fly box and produced his Monstrosity which he tied onto his cast. I nearly fell out of the boat on seeing the colour and size of it and said, 'How can you expect to catch a fish on that in these hot calm conditions?' He laughed and proceeded to waterproof the fly. This was a puzzler, as he had a sinking line rigged on his rod and I wondered what sort of tactics he was going to employ.

He cast this thing out and stripped it back. With the sinking line and greased up fly all you could see was the Monstrosity scuttling across the mirror calm surface of the lake. The sinking line had taken the fly leader under, so there was no sign of any drag. On his second cast there was a splash and he had a fish on and after about half an hour he had his limit in the bag using this technique. Meanwhile I had acquired a tying off him and I soon had my limit bag in the boat.

This pattern has worked for Arnold on other waters just as effectively and I think this is why he is always in the news catching big fish or winning competitions. The odd and weird dressings he pulls out of his fly box have to be seen to be believed; however he is a very skilled flyfisherman and can hold his own against the very best.

I have since used this greased fly on sinking line technique with big dapping flies and large muddlers and on its day it is very effective way of taking trout.

Arnold's Monstrosity
Tag　Orange wool
Body　Peacock herl lightly dressed
Body hackle　Blue dun cock
Hackle　Black and white cock wound together
Hook　Size 10 mayfly

Parachute Hackle Flies

A great many of the fly patterns given in this chapter are suitable to be dressed with the hackle wound on a horizontal plane. Flies so dressed are known as parachute hackle flies. This is an especially good method for dressing the spinners of the upwinged flies with the wings in the spent or semi-spent position; they are certainly very effective.

There are special hooks designed to be dressed with the hackle on the horizontal plane. However over the years these hooks come and go and the design keeps changing; it would appear there have been many design faults and, as far as I am aware none have really stood the test of time.

Many tying techniques can be employed to achieve the horizontally wound hackle but a great number are time-consuming and tiresome to dress. For the tyer who is skilled and has the knowledge, the rewards of good fishing which comes when fishing the dry parachute hackled patterns more than make up for the time spent tying them.

A quick method for dressing a parachute hackled fly is as follows:

1　Place a hook in the vice as normal.
2　Wind the silk down the hookshank and tie in the tail fibres if required.
3　Complete body in the normal fashion.
4　Select two hackles for wings, prepare and tie them in an upright position.
5　Tie in quality cock hackle in front of wings, flat so that the barbs are in line with hookshank, thereby making it possible for the hackle to be wound horizontally. Use a hackle slightly longer in the barb than you would use for a traditional style dry fly.
6　Wind the hackle horizontally around the wing base; when enough turns have been taken, secure hackle tip.
7　Part hackle wings with finger and thumb and press them down into the spent

position; this will force the hackle outwards and down. Secure with figure of eight whipping, complete head and varnish.

This is a good method of dressing for running water as the flies float well in this environment. During hot calm days on still water when the film on the water becomes very thick, this mode of dressing is not as effective because the hook point fails to penetrate the film, thus tipping the fly on its side. This does not occur however, when there is a good breeze which causes plenty of ripple and movement in the water's surface.

Another technique for dressing the hackle horizontally requires the use of what is called a 'gallows' tool. This tool is fitted onto the fly-tying vice stem; when it is in position it looks just like a hangman's gallows with the gibbet in position over the vice jaws and its wire spring and hook hanging down. I have modified my gallows tool with rubber bands: I find this much more convenient to work with.

The most effective parachute fly in my view is tied in the spent position using the following method and making use of the gallows tool. The object of this method is to dress a spinner with the hook-point pointing up towards the sky when the fly is on the water.

1   Place down-eyed hook in vice; whip on silk foundation, tie in tail fibres. Select stiff hair, stiff guard hair or horse tail hair, hair from moose or perhaps some bucktail will be suitable.
2   Tie in three hairs for the tail, separating one from the other with a turn of silk so that they fan out on a horizontal plane. Take advantage of any natural curve in the hair and tie in so that the curve bends down the same way as the hook. The tail fibres are very important in helping the fly float with the hook point upwards.
3   Dress the body and tie the hackle in horizontally. Take a piece of nylon line ten pounds breaking strain and three inches long. Tie this in just behind where the wing would be tied in. Form a loop with the nylon line and secure the end with a couple of turns of silk.
4   Turn the hook in the vice, point upwards. Tie in hackle wings in a spent or semi-spent position; turn hook the correct way up in the vice. Move the gallows tool into position and hook up the nylon loop. This will give it support and keep it taut while the hackle is being wound. Wind hackle, remove gallows tool hook, at the same time keeping pressure on the loop with your fingers; pass the hackle tip and loose end of nylon line through the loop. Pull the other end of nylon line tight thus securing the hackle in position.
5   Secure loose nylon line ends, cut off and whip finish.

The end product of this mode is the ultimate in dry flies. Having the hook bend and point turned up in the air ensures the horizontally wound hackle barbs gives a very realistic imprint on the water's surface and very much like the real thing when viewed from below. A spinner so dressed is much more effective than a fly of the same pattern dressed in the traditional style. There is a little problem I have found with this mode of parachute dressing, in that sometimes it will land on the water upside down. What causes this to happen I am not sure, it could be bad casting or perhaps the weight of the hook point. I would suggest that when tying on the fly, the bottom of the hackle which sits on the water is facing the angler while being tied on to the cast. Also ensure there are no twists or kinks in fly line or leader.

The best method I found to present the parachute fly is to cast normally, but instead of placing the fly on the water in the normal way cast to a point a couple of feet above the water's surface. Once the fly has finished travelling forward, it will gently float down on the water. If you are covering a fish in this sort of situation, the response of the trout to the fly as it alights on the water can be sudden and explosive, the ultimate in dry fly fishing.

The sedge patterns given can be dressed in this mode and use made of the horns to help to balance the fly. Instead of a clipped deer hair body I would select a couple of long hairs from a bucktail and wind them on the hookshank to form a body. Bucktail hair used for body material makes for a very light fly which floats well.

'On their sides' Sedges

I have developed another tying technique for my sedge patterns, dressing the hook in such a way that it lies on its side in the surface film while being used. The hackle is deer hair and body colour the colour of whatever silk is being used.

To dress my 'on their sides' sedges:

1 Place the hook in the vice as normal.

2 Wind silk two thirds down the hookshank.

3 Tie in a piece of marabou floss, binding in loose end two thirds down hookshank.

4 Make a loop out of the marabou floss on the side of hookshank facing you, secure the floss with a couple of turns of silk leaving loose end pointing out past the hookeye.

5 Turn the hook upside down in the vice and tie in a pair of hackles of a type normally used for flat wings on sedges on the side of hook facing you, making sure the stalks are left to form the horns.

6 Turn hook correct way up. Check the floss loop is functioning by gently pulling the loose end and at the same time putting scissor points into the loop to avoid it pulling through or out.

7 Prepare the deer hair for the hackle. First cut a bunch of deer hair to the length required. A good guide is to have it slightly longer than the hookshank of hook being dressed.

8 Split the deer hair bunch into two, turn one half the opposite way and place the bunch back together again. This should give roughly the same number of cut and fine ends of hair at each end of the bunch. The hair hackle is now ready for tying in.

9 Insert the hair into the floss loop, holding both between finger and thumb, pull the loop gently. When tight enough to hold the hair, open the finger and thumb, at the same time pulling the loop tight and pressing on the hair centre with the thumb. This action will cause the deer hair to flare out vertically on the hookshank side thus forming the deer hackle. Complete with whip finish and varnish, taking care to varnish the centre of the hair hackle which will help it stay in place.

The easy way to handle the deer hair when preparing hackles is to cut the top off an old pen slightly shorter than the hackle required. Place one bunch of hair in the pen top and the other bunch the other way. Give the pen top a couple of taps on the table; this will ensure the hair is mixed and the ends are all lined up. All the tyer needs to do now is to take the hair out of the pen top and tie in.

The only problem I have had with this style of dressing is that when fishing with it, it is not possible to be sure what side it is going to land on, wing or hackle. However it does not appear to make much difference to the fish, they take it well. If possible use straight eyed hooks for the on the side mode; down- or up-eyed hooks do not suit it.

Grouse Wine Sedge
Tying silk   Brown
Hackle   Natural deer hair
Wings   Woodcock hackles
Hook   Size 12, longshank

Mottled Sedge (*Plate 9*)
Tying silk   Brown
Hackle   Deer hair, speckle marked with felt pen (green)
Wing   Reddish brown pheasant edged with black
Hook   Size 12, longshank

Large Red Sedge
Tying Silk   Claret
Hackle   Deer hair
Wing   Reddish brown pheasant edged with black
Hook   Size 12, longshank

Grey Sedge
Tying Silk   White
Hackle   Deer hair
Wing   Grey partridge or grey mallard flank
Hook   Size 12, longshank
The hackle stalks can be left to form horns.

Detached Body Parachute Hackled Dry Flies

Another useful addition to the dry fly angler's armoury is the detached body parachute hackled dry fly. This is a very light mode of dressing and is not very durable, but very successful when it comes to taking fish; perhaps it is not as good as the hook up in the air variety but it is considerably easier to dress.

To dress the detached body version, first place a hook in the vice in the normal fashion. Wind the silk half way down the hookshank. To prepare the tail and body, take a grey mallard flank feather; the size of feather will be determined by the size of fly being dressed. Hold the feather by the stalk (depending what length the twin tails are required), cut the hackle stalk at the top. This will leave a vee in the top of the hackle. Allowing the twin tails to be two or three fibres wide, now strip off the fibres at the bottom of hackle stalk, leaving about half a dozen fibres each side of the stalk to form the fly body. Parting the body fibres from the tail fibres, pull them down the hackle stalk to form the detached body. Tie the hackle stalk and fibres in halfway on the hookshank. Trim off surplus stalk and fibres and secure. Now tie in two hackle wings in the upright position. Tie in the hackle horizontally and wind around the base of wings, part wings into semi-spent position and secure with figure of eight whipping. Now complete head and varnish.

All dry fly patterns so far given can be dressed in this detached mode. For the different body and tail colours use natural or dyed hackles of the following birds: partridge, pheasant, mallard and teal.

The Water Boatman (*Plate 9*)
Hook   Wide gape size 10
Body   Black tying silk
Hackle   Black hackle
Dress the boatman using the hookpoint in the air mode. This makes a very good imitation of the boatman and allows it to be fished in a very realistic manner.

I have designed these dry flies using only hair – no feather fibres whatsoever. Realistically, the smallest hook that can be used to dress hair flies with parachute deerhair hackles is size twelve wide gape or size fourteen mayfly. A really skilled tyer may be able to go smaller, however I see no point in doing so and I would then change to feathers.

Large Red Sedge
Body   Three hairs brown bucktail wound
Wing   Red squirrel tail hair (sparsely dressed)
Hackle   Deer hair natural

Brown Sedge
Body   Three dyed orange hairs from bucktail
Wing   Brown bucktail
Hackle   Deer hair natural

Black Sedge
Body   Three dyed black hairs from bucktail
Wing   Grey brown bucktail
Hackle   Dyed black deer hair

Yellow Dung Fly
Body   Three dyed yellow hairs from bucktail
Wing   Grey brown bucktail
Hackle   Dyed yellow and natural deer hair mixed

Grey Sedge
Body   White and grey bucktail
Wing   Grey brown bucktail
Hackle   Grey bucktail

The all-hair flies are good floaters and fish well in a big wave, particularly when dressed in the larger hook size.

The mode of dressing is the same as on the side sedges for the hair hackles, otherwise dress them in the normal manner, hookpoint downwards.

5

The Wet Fly

Wet flies are probably the most important fly type for the fly-fisher. I have devised a range of flies which have stood the test of time to try and cover every aspect of fishing flies wet. My list of dressings range from pupa tyings to imitate the naturals to the fancy colourful dressings which look like nothing natural on earth. However all the patterns on their day will take fish; it is up to the angler to recognise the signs and fish the correct fly for the conditions prevailing at the time.

Blue Dun
Tail   Coot or moorhen hackle fibres
Body   Yellow seal's fur
Thorax   Mole fur
Wing cases   Coot or moorhen
Hackle   Coot (one turn)
Hook   Size 8, 10, 12, 14, 16, wide gape

On the Tamar system the blue dun and iron blues appear in large numbers, so this pattern can be very effective. I prefer the size twelve hook (although I have taken fish on size sixteen) as I think the larger hook sinks a little better in the faster flowing water. However the fly can be leaded, but I really don't think that is necessary.

Black and Peacock – *Standard Pattern*
Body   Peacock herl
Hackle   Black hen
Hook   Size 8, 10, 12, 14, wide gape

When tying herls of any kind always twist them into a rope with the tying silk and wind them together up the shank to form the body.

Black and Peacock Silver Tip
Tag   Silver flat tinsel
Body   Peacock herl from peacock eye
Hackle   Blue black hackle from melanistic pheasant

This is basically a variation of the Black and Peacock; they are both good imitations of the common aquatic snails. Snails, where they exist, form part of the trout's diet and are normally browsed off weed or the bed of the lake. During mid or late summer a mass migration of snails to the surface takes place; although I have only observed this twice it is a most interesting phenomenon. They float in their shells just under the surface film as they are able to stick their foot or pad onto the underside of the film. They can be carried like this in whatever direction the wind or current of the water takes them, or they can move quite quickly by their own efforts using the foot or pad. The snails will remain on the surface for days.

For the angler this is a golden opportunity, for when the snails are up the trout will feed on them and become most selective and are unlikely to be taken on anything other than a floating snail imitation. If the angler does not have a floating snail imitation handy, an all black deer bodied sedge pattern or the ordinary Black and Peacock, waterproofed and fished on the surface, will take fish.

Caddis *(Plate 10)*
Body Leaded, overtied with peacock herl backed with cock pheasant tail fibres
Hackle Natural brown hen
Cheeks Feather slips from hen pheasant wing quills
Head Peacock herl
Hook Size 6, 8, wide gape

The cheeks are wing quill slips tied in short each side of hookshank in front of the hackle, thus forming short stubby wings under the body with the wing tips pointed towards the hook barb.

Sedge Pupa No 1
Body First third from hook bend yellow D.F.M. wool, remainder peacock herl
Back Pheasant tail fibres
Hackle Natural red cock
Head Peacock herl
Hook Size 6, 8, 10, wide gape

Sedge Pupa No 2 *(Plate 10)*
Body First third orange D.F.M. wool, remainder peacock herl
Back, hackle, head and hook same as No 1

Sedge Pupa No 3
Body First third lime D.F.M. wool, remainder peacock herl
Back, hackle, head and hook same as No 1.

All three dressings are very useful patterns on lakes during the season. A friend, Chris Martindale, did very well at Colliford Lake fishing for brown trout using sedge pupa number three.

The Longhorn Nymph Series

Green Longhorn *(Plate 10)*
Tying Silk Red
Body D.F.M. yellow wool and D.F.M. green wool mixed and dubbed on silk
Horns Cock golden pheasant centre tail fibres
Hackle Grey partridge

Amber Longhorn
Body Yellow and orange seal's fur mixed
Silk, horns and hackle same as green longhorn

Yellow Longhorn
Body Yellow seal's fur
Silk, horns and hackle same as green longhorn

Orange Longhorn
Body Orange Seal's Fur
Silk, horns and hackle same as green longhorn

Useful dressings when the longhorn and silverhorns are in the margins and are being blown out onto the water.

Orange D.F.M. Spider
Body   Orange D.F.M. floss over black silk
Rib   Size 14 gold oval tinsel
Hackle   Furnace hen (well marked)
Hook   Size 10, 12, 14, wide gape

I have, on most occasions, always done quite well with this good brown trout fly, particularly on lakes when a big wave is blowing up. Just stand well back from the bank and fish the first two yards of water from the shore.

Grizzle and Peacock
Tail   Grizzle cock hackle fibres
Body   Herl from peacock's eye
Hackle   Grizzle (barred Plymouth Rock cock)
Hook   Size 10, 12, 14, wide gape

Useful for June and August on the river, probably taken for some sort of beetle. If you substitute the herl for a stripped quill and a grizzle body hackle you will have a very useful dry fly.

I first met Arnold Curtis at Siblyback Lake in 1970. He is a very good angler and a keen fly-tyer; we exchanged views on our sport and this was the start of a long friendship.

In August 1973 we were sharing a boat at Crowdy Marsh Lake, Camelford. It was very quiet and very hot, not much was happening. Digging around in our fly boxes looking for a pattern that would interest the fish, Arnold came up with his green tag dressing, the only one he had; he had the same pattern with an orange tag which I tried.

It was amazing, he just could not go wrong and within an hour he had his limit. Up to now I had not touched a fish, so taking the fly from Arnold I tied it on my leader and in even less time I had my limit, a beautiful bag of rainbow trout. It is a very effective dressing and since it was devised there have been quite a few new dressings incorporating the D.F.M. green wool as a tag.

Arnold's Green Tag – *(A. Curtis)* – *(Plate 10)*
Tag   D.F.M. green wool
Body   Peacock herl
Body hackle   Blue dun cock
Hackle   Black cock
Hook   Size 8, 10, longshank

Woodcock and D.F.M. Yellow
Tail   Woodcock hackle fibres
Body   Yellow seal's fur mixed with D.F.M. yellow wool
Rib   Size 15 gold oval tinsel
Hackle   Woodcock

Woodcock and Claret *(Plate 10)*
Tying silk   Bright red
Tail   Woodcock hackle fibres
Body   Dark claret seal's fur
Rib   Size 15 gold oval tinsel
Hackle   Woodcock
Head   Red silk
Hook   Size 8, 10, 12, wide gape

Two effective patterns that will take trout right through the fishing season. The claret version is extremely good on moorland waters and it is deadly on the new big water at Colliford, which has only wild brown trout. The D.F.M. yellow version has a shorter season on the moorland waters but it is still a very useful pattern to carry.

Pheasant Tag Series

The Pheasant Tag series can be dressed on any size hook ranging from sizes 4, 6, 8, 10, 12, wide gape.

Remember when tying herls to twist them around the tying silk and then wind, which will improve the durability of the dressings. These dressings are useful on both lake and river and have quite a long season.

Black Pheasant Red Tag
Tail   Red wool
Body   Black seal's fur, ribbed silver oval tinsel
Thorax   Pinch of red wool dubbed on silk
Hackle   Melanistic pheasant neck

Pheasant Green Tag
Tail   Lime green wool
Body   Pheasant centre tail fibres
Thorax   Pinch of lime green wool
Hackle   Reddish brown pheasant feather edged with black

Black Pheasant Orange Tag
Tail   Orange wool
Body   Melanistic centre tail fibres
Thorax   Pinch of orange wool
Hackle   Melanistic pheasant neck

Pheasant Yellow Tag
Tail   Yellow wool
Body   Pheasant centre tail
Thorax   Pinch of yellow wool
Hackle   Reddish brown pheasant feather edged with black

Blue Teal
Tail   Blue wool
Body   Blue underfur of rabbit
Rib   Size 16 oval silver tinsel
Body hackle   White cock
Hackle   Teal flank dressed as collar and swept back

Magenta Mallard
Tail   D.F.M. magenta wool
Body   Red seal's fur
Rib   Size 16 oval gold tinsel
Body hackle   Claret cock
Hackle   Brown mallard shoulder second dressed as collar and swept back

Two deadly patterns for rainbow trout, useful for sea trout also. Hook sizes 6 or 8, wide gape.

Waterhen Series

Waterhen and Red *(Plate 10)*
Body   Black seal's fur
Rib   Oval silver tinsel
Thorax   Red seal's fur
Hackle   Feather from waterhen wing

On the Waterhen Series the colour of seal's fur for the thorax can be changed to yellow, green, orange, purple and magenta to give a wide range of options to the angler. Hook sizes: 8, 10, 12, wide gape.

Dung Fly *(Plate 10)*
Body   Bright yellow seal's fur
Rib   Gold oval tinsel
Hackle   Woodcock
Hook   Size 8, 10, 12, 14, wide gape

Amber Yellow Fly
Body   In two parts: back end – bright yellow seal's fur; front end – amber seal's fur
Rib   Size 16 gold oval tinsel
Hackle   Woodcock
Hook   Size 8 or 10, wide gape

Orange Yellow Fly
Body   In two parts: back end – Naples yellow seal's fur; front end – orange seal's fur
Rib   Size 16 gold oval tinsel
Hackle   Woodcock

From early June onwards when the cow dung fly is on the water the Dung Fly, Amber Yellow Fly and Orange Yellow Fly can be very effective – sometimes a little pinch of olive seal's fur in the yellow part of the dubbing could make a difference on some days.

Pheasant Tail Series

The pheasant tail series are a useful weapon in the fly-fisher's armoury; they will take fish in all water and virtually at any time if the temperature is suitable. The hook sizes are 8, 10, 12, 14, wide gape

Pheasant Tail
Tail   Cock pheasant centre tail fibres
Body   Cock pheasant tail fibres
Thorax   Hare's ear
Wing cases   Pheasant tail

Hare's Face
Tail   Cock pheasant tail
Body   Hare's fur
Rib   Gold oval tinsel
Thorax   Pinch of yellow seal's fur
Hackle   Reddish brown pheasant edged with black

Golden Pheasant Tail
Tail   Golden pheasant tail fibres
Body   Golden pheasant tail fibres

Plate 9: Trout Dry Flies (see Chapter 4)

Daddy-Longlegs No. 1
Cinnamon Sedge

Daddy-Longlegs No. 2
Mottled Sedge

Daddy-Longlegs No. 3
Large Red Sedge

Mottle Sedge Parachute: 'on the side' style

Red Quill: parachute hackle and detached body

Blue-winged Olive: parachute hackle and detached body

Ginger Quill: parachute hackle with hood point up in the air

Water-boatman: parachute hackle with hook point up in the air

Grouse Wing Sedge: 'on the side' style

Plate 10: Trout Wet Flies (see Chapter 5)

Rabbit	Purple and Gold	Grey Phantom Nymph	Hatching Grey Phantom Nymph
Corixa	Green Longhorn	Woodcock and Claret	Caddis
Waterhen and Red	Half Stonefly	Red Pupa	Dung Fly

Red Double P	Green Woolley No. 1	Red-Eyed Beetle
Renegade	Arnold's Green Tag	Stick Fly
Dragonfly Nymph	Stickleback	Sedge Pupa No. 2

Plate 11: Sea Trout Flies (see Chapter 7)

Red Mallard and Claret	Ramsbottom's Favourite	Freeman's Fancy
Teal and Orange	Lady Inny	Depth Charge
Lord Penpont	Coachman	Heckham and Peckham
Lady Gwen	Lady Luck	Teal and Black
Yellow Fly		The Keeper
Green Minnow		Peacock Fly

Plate 12: Sea Trout Two Hook Lures (see Chapter 7)

Claret and Mallard
Silver Blue Lure
Dunkeld Lure
Butcher Lure
Tubes: Red Flashabou Tube

Silver Grey Lure
Silver Ghost Lure
Alexandra Lure
Dirty Water Lure
Blue Flashabou Tube

Thorax   Blue underfur of rabbit
Wing cases   Golden pheasant

Melanistic Pheasant Tail
Tail   Black pheasant tail fibres
Body   Black pheasant tail fibres
Thorax   Mole fur
Wing cases   Blue jay

Orange Pheasant Tail
Tail   Dyed orange pheasant tail fibres
Body   Pheasant tail fibres
Thorax   Ginger rabbit fur
Wing cases   Dyed orange pheasant

In September 1986 I took my biggest brown trout on fly with the Corixa at Colliford Lake. I had cast well out giving the fly time to sink, then slowly began to retrieve it in. Everything went solid and for a moment I thought I had hooked one of the many gorse bushes which cover the lake bed. But then it took off and I knew I was into a fish, a good one at that; the fish stayed about twenty yards out cruising from side to side. Gradually I played it in and after about five minutes it was beaten and safely netted by Chris Martindale. It was a beautiful well marked wild fish of 3 lbs 9 ozs.

Corixa *(Plate 10)*
Tag   Silver tinsel
Body   White rabbit fur mixed with a pinch of yellow seal's fur
Rib   Size 16 oval silver tinsel
Back   Feather slip from woodcock quill
Hackle   Woodcock
Hook   Size 8 or 10, wide gape.

The fly can be leaded if required and can be used right through the season.

Bloodworm
Tail   Red rubber band
Body   Leaded, overtied with red floss
Thorax   Dyed red ostrich herl
Hook   Size 8, 10, wide gape

When tying in the rubber band use the natural curve of the band to ensure that it curves upwards, rather like a hound's tail does when it is running on the scent.

Black Pupa
Tail   White cock fibres
Body   Black goose herl
Rib   Gold wire
Thorax   Peacock herl
Breathing tubes   White cock fibres

The Black Pupa was the first fly I ever tied, and the first I caught a fish on. I used a pair of locking pliers called mole-grips as I did not have a vice. Into these pliers I locked the hook and dressed the fly. The end result was a bit crude but I tried it one day while fishing. I cast it out, saw a swirl, lifted the rod, hooked and duly landed a nice brown trout – quite an experience, I shall never forget it.

Red Pupa *(Plate 10)*
Tail   White cock fibres
Body   Dyed red goose herl
Rib   Gold wire
Thorax   Peacock herl
Hook   Size 10, 12, 14, 16, wide gape

When tying the pupa take the tying silk and wind it right down to the bend of the hook before tying in the white cock fibres.

Pupa Dressings

The chironomid midge pupae vary in size and colour. When conditions are suitable they come to the surface of the water to emerge. They have a segmented body and appendages at the tail which help to propel the pupae. These appendages are transparent which gives a distinct whitish tinge to the tail end. On arrival at the surface they sometimes have difficulty getting through the surface film; this is most likely to happen on a hot calm evening when the density of the surface film will keep a large number of pupae hanging there, thus causing a large rise of trout. It is not so easy to take advantage of this rise as the trout become very selective so it is important to fish the right colour pupae by examining the hatching midges and seeing what colour they are. The pupae can be claret, black, red, green, yellow, orange and brown colour and the midges from them start appearing as a rule from late April onwards.

To tie the standard pupa dressing, wind the silk from hookeye down the shank and halfway down the bend. Take a bunch of white cock hackle fibres, lay them on the hookshank so that each end of the fibres form the head breathing tubes and the tail end appendages. Securely cover the fibres with turns of silk. Assuming the silk colour is correct for the pattern being tied, now tie in the peacock herl at the hookeye end and wind to form the thorax. If the silk colour is correct the pupa is now completed. Cut off the white cock fibres at the head and tail so that the breathing tubes and tail appendages are about 0.5 cm/¼ in long. If a rib is required use silver or gold wire to give the segmented effect to the body; some tyers use white silk or a stripped cock hackle stalk.

Red Pupa – *Standard Pattern*
Tying silk   Red
Tail   White cock fibres
Body   Red silk
Rib   Silver wire
Thorax   Peacock herl
Breathing tubes   White cock fibres
Hook   Size 10, 12, 14, 16, wide gape

It is quite easy to spot trout feeding on hatching chironomid pupae because of the distinctive rise form, a slow nose to tail rise with the dorsal fin and tail fin breaking the surface of the water. The only other time trout will rise in this manner is when they are taking floating snails or caenis.

There are many methods of presenting the hatching midge pupae: some anglers will grease their leaders to within an inch or two of the pupae, having two or three artificials on the cast, fishing them slowly so that they hang in the surface film. Another method is to fish three artificials on the same cast using a very long leader of some 4–4.5 m/12–14 ft. Cast the flies out and leave them to sink before retrieving them back at a speed so that all three artificials are fishing at different depths. I prefer to fish with a sedge pattern on the point well waterproofed and a pupae on the dropper; using this method I have had some success. It requires great concentration and the floating sedge must be carefully watched; at the sign of any movement tighten immediately and usually any trout that has taken the artificial pupae is hooked. If there is a ripple on the water there is no need to move the flies, the bobbing up and down of the sedge will impart all the movement needed – all the angler needs to do is keep a taut line and avoid any slack. When fishing in this manner trout will sometimes hook themselves and on occasions I have had the sedge itself taken with a splashy rise.

Large hatches of caenis occur just before sunset and when the trout become pre-occupied on broadwings the angler should have little difficulty in recognizing the quick nose and tail rise of a trout so engaged. They will on occasions accept a lure stripped across their noses or a large dry sedge. However when they are on the water in massive numbers it is very difficult and frustrating for the angler, so the pattern given below will prove productive at such times:

Anglers Curse
Body White tying silk covering only half of the hookshank
Hackle Light blue hen
Hook Size 16, 18, 20, wide gape.

D.F.M. Yellow Nymph
Body Strand of D.F.M. yellow floss
Rib Silver wire
Head Dyed olive ostrich herl
Hook Size 12, 14, 16, wide gape

Stonefly
Body Hare fur and yellow seal's fur mixed
Rib Gold wire
Body hackle Grizzle
Hackle Waterhen
Hook Size 10, 12, 14, wide gape

Half Stonefly *(Plate 10)*
Body Yellow seal's fur
Rib Gold oval tinsel or wire
Hackle Waterhen
Hook Size 10, 12, 14, wide gape

The stonefly and half-stonefly I have designed to be fished wet; if used when the stoneflies are in season but when there is no apparent surface activity they will take fish. When the stoneflies are on the water the wet versions very often are more effective than the dry patterns.

Shrimp Patterns

Freshwater shrimp are common in most waters and I believe there are several species. The colour will vary from translucent grey to an orange brown during the mid-summer breeding season. They prefer rocky bottoms or weed beds which will give them some cover from the marauding trout; this is the sort of water for the angler to fish the artificial using the sink and draw method.

The Shrimp No 1
Body　Leaded to form a hump
Hackles　Two or three olive hackles tied in and wound down body. Trim excess hackle
　　fibres from side of body
Wing Cases　Clear P.V.C. Bring over body and tie in
Rib　Orange floss
Head　Olive ostrich herl
Hook　Size 10, 12, wide gape

The Shrimp No 2
Body　Leaded to form a hump; form body with orange ostrich herl
Rib　Gold oval tinsel
Hackles　Two natural orange hackles wound down body and trimmed at sides
Wing Cases　Clear raffia
Hook　Size 10, 12, wide gape

The Shrimp No 3
Body　Leaded to form a hump, then dub olive and red mixture of seal's fur – 60% to 40%
Rib　Gold oval tinsel
Hackles　Two natural orange hackles wound down body and trimmed at sides
Hook　Size 10, 12, wide gape

I have used the term wing cases for the shrimps, which is not strictly accurate – however I am sure this will give the reader a more clear mental image of what to try to dress. Shrimp dressing number three can be dressed with a dark green raffia back, or call it wing cases if you wish.

Freshwater Louse
Body　Pale olive seal's fur
Rib　Silver wire
Hackles　Grey partridge
Hook　Size 12, 14, wide gape

This small crustacean is quite common and is found in all types of stillwater. They are closely related to shrimp and are very often found in company with them; unlike the shrimp they prefer bottom vegetation rather than the rocks and weed beds. As the natural is usually found in the shallows probably the best way of fishing the artificial is to use a floating fly line, a short leader allowing the fly to sink, and move it slowly along the lake bottom in short jerks.

Large Red Water Mite
Body　Leaded, dressed red seal's fur
Rib　Silver wire
Hackle　Blue black pheasant
Hook　Size 12, 14, 16, 18, wide gape

March Brown
Body　Yellow seal's fur
Rib　Silver oval tinsel
Hackle　Dark partridge or quail
Wing　Hen pheasant dressed slim
Hook　Size 10, 12, 14, 16, wide gape

A good early season fly particularly in the larger sizes.

Dragonfly Nymph *(Plate 10)*
Tail Grey partridge hackle fibres
Body Grannon and green highlander seal's fur mixed 75% to 25%
Rib Gold oval tinsel
Hackle Grey partridge wound as collar and swept back
Head Peacock herl with two red beads tied as eyes
Hook Size 6, 8, 10, longshank

Red-eyed Beetle *(Plate 10)*
Tail Pheasant tail fibres
Body Leaded – peacock herl
Wing cases Pheasant tail fibres
Hackle Brown partridge
Head Two red beads
Hook Size 8, 10, wide gape

Sticklebacks and the fry of other fish provide a useful food item for some trout in still waters. Usually in the summer the small fish congregate in large shoals in the margins of lakes and it is at this time the trout become preoccupied with the abundance of food. I have been on the banks of lakes when the water only a few feet out erupts with small fish trying to escape the trout, which hang about out in the deeper water and make regular forays in the margins. When this happens tie the artificial on and when the trout makes one of his runs in try and fish it in front of him. The opportunity to do this does not present itself very often and the only other method is to fish the artificial in the deeper water drawing it into the shallows in an attractive manner; pause for a moment after fishing out a cast before lifting off and casting again. Very often trout will seize it just as it breaks the surface: I once had a rainbow trout of over six pounds do this to me. When this happens the fish comes at it in such an explosive manner that the hard take and the splash that follows gives one quite a start, no matter how prepared you are. When fishing a fry imitation it is important to mount an artificial which corresponds nearest to the natural fry in the water at the time; the angler who copies the actions of the natural will, if the size and colour is right, always take fish.

Stickleback *(Plate 10)*
Tail Two olive cock hackles tied back to back trimmed to fish tail shape
Body Silver tinsel, overwound with clear PVC
Rib Red wool, to a fish like shape
Hackle Olive cock dressed as collar and swept back over body
Head Two white beads with peacock herl around them thus giving the appearance of eyes
  set in the head
Hook Size 4, 6, 8, longshank

Cut the PVC into narrow strips for tying – when winding it to form the body gently stretch it and this will give a very neat tight translucent body.

The Dam Buster and Green Tag were firm favourites at Siblyback Lake and my wife used to tie up large numbers of them for the local anglers.

Siblyback Dam Buster
Tag D.F.M. scarlet wool
Body Peacock herl
Hackle Long fibre furnace cock dressed as collar and then swept back, thus veiling the
  body
Hook Size 8, 10, longshank

Siblyback D.F.M. Green Tag
Tail D.F.M. green wool
Body Black wool
Hackle Long fibre black cock swept back veiling the body
Head Brown chenille
Hook Size 8, 10, longshank

The large black cock hackle for the green tag should be tied in close to the hookeye and wound, then the hackle fibres swept towards the tail and overtied; now tie the chenille in, thus forming a large muddler type head. If properly tied the cock hackle fibres should veil the fly body so that when it is fished through the water in short jerks, life is imparted to the fly. It pays sometimes to change the colour of the hackle: a very useful variation is tied with brown cock fibre tail, orange wool body and a large dyed yellow cock hackle.

Renegade *(Plate 10)*
Body Peacock herl lightly dressed
Body Hackle Natural red cock
Rib Dark green floss
Hackle Natural red cock
Hook Size 10, longshank

This pattern has proved very effective for rainbows in stillwater and at times deadly when greased up and fished dry in a big wave. Sometimes stripping it across the surface in rough conditions like a wake fly will take fish.

Alder Fly
Body Peacock herl dyed magenta
Wing Woodcock
Hackle Blue-black pheasant
Hook Size 10, 12, wide gape

Red Alder
Body Claret and magenta seal's fur
Rib Peacock herl overtied with red silk
Hackle Coot

Colliford Fly
Body Cock pheasant tail fibres dyed yellow
Thorax Pinch of D.F.M. yellow wool
Hackle Moorhen
Hook Size 10, 12, wide gape

Heather Fly Series

All the heather flies have blue-black pheasant hackles, seal's fur bodies ribbed with silver oval tinsel. Hook size 8, 10, 12, wide gape. The heather fly is a terrestrial species of the same family as the hawthorne. It is in season longer than the hawthorne and normally seen during August and September. The heather fly can be easily identified as it has a reddish colour to its underside.

Red Heather Fly
Body In three parts: black – red – black
Rib Silver oval tinsel

Yellow Heather Fly
Body In three parts: black – yellow – black

Orange Heather Fly
Body In three parts: black – orange – black

Green Heather Fly
Body In three parts: black – green – black

Yellow Sally
Body Yellow seal's fur
Rib Gold wire
Body hackle White cock
Hackle Grey partridge dyed yellow
Hook Size 12, 14, 16, wide gape

Useful throughout the season when the stoneflies are on the wing – usually April to August; on the river they are most common during June and July. Not normally seen on still water.

Willow Fly
Body Hare's ear, red and yellow seal's fur mixed
Rib Gold wire
Hackle Brown partridge
Hook Size 12, 14, wide gape

The willow fly is a late season species most common during August and September. Hatches are often quite heavy on rivers, but I have never seen much of them on still waters probably because the hatches are more spread out on the large expanse of water.

Beetle Dressings

The beetles are a very large group and I have selected the most common species of which I have devised artificials. The soldier and sailor beetles appear in June, July and August in large numbers and if they are blown out onto the water in sufficient numbers it is well worth fishing the artificial. The fall of beetles, like ants, is likely to occur in the middle of a warm day. The coch-y-bonddu is a beetle which appears in large numbers in June and is often blown onto the water; in some areas it is known as the June bug or bracken clock. I have not devised a dressing for it as the standard pattern would be very difficult to improve on.

Red Double P *(Plate 10)*
Tag Red wool
Body Peacock herl
Thorax Pinch of seal's fur
Hackle Reddish brown pheasant with black edge
Eyes Two red beads
Hook Size 8, 10, wide gape

A useful beetle dressing; I have done well with it at Crowdy March Lake.

Black Beetle
Body Black chenille

Back Blue-green slip from magpie tail
Hackle Blue-black pheasant
Hook Size 8, 10, wide gape

Soldier Beetle
Body Orange chenille
Back Pheasant tail fibres
Hackle Reddish-brown pheasant hackle with black edge
Hook Size 8, 10, wide gape

Sailor Beetle
Body Brown chenille
Back Blue-green slip from magpie tail
Hackle Blue-black pheasant
Hook Size 8, 10, wide gape

Green Woolley No 1 *(Plate 10)*
Body Green chenille
Body hackle White cock clipped on top
Head Peacock herl
Eyes Two red beads
Hook Size 6, 8, longshank

Green Woolley No 2
Body Green chenille
Body hackle Green highlander clipped on top
Head Peacock herl
Eyes Two red beads
Hook Size 6, 8, longshank

The Rabbit *(Plate 10)*
Body Blue rabbit underfur
Rib Silver wire
Wing Hen pheasant – short stubby each side of hookshank
Hackle Rabbit guard hair
Hook Size 8, 10, wide gape

To tie a hair hackle: make a loop in the tying silk; secure the open end of loop to hookshank; spread rabbit fur in loop; twist the silk thus trapping the fur between it, now wind it like a hackle and tie in. Trim off surplus fur on the hair hackle. It should now look like a deer hair muddler type head but considerably narrower.

Purple and Gold *(Plate 10)*
Body Purple seal's fur
Body hackle Red cock
Rib Gold oval tinsel
Hackle Brown partridge
Hook Size 8, 10, wide gape

Useful for rough streams and fast water.

Nymphs and Hatching Nymphs

Grey Phantom Nymph *(Plate 10)*
Silk White
Body Grey herl

Rib Silver wire
Thorax Stone-coloured hare's fur
Wing cases Grey feather strip
Hook Size 12, 14, wide gape

The herl for the bodies can be taken from any grey feather; I find herl taken from a grey goose is very suitable and easy to handle. The hare's fur will come from the underside of the hare; I don't think the colour needs to be exact for the thorax as long as it is as near as it is possible to get.

The adult grey midge can be observed on the water during the summer months sometimes in large quantities; it is a little smaller than the black midge. When on the water it appears to be a light grey colour; if you examine it you will see the body is almost translucent with a greenish tinge. The nymph has an almost transparent body and the trout will feed mainly on them while they are hatching on the surface. The adult midge are also taken at this time. To increase the angler's chances when a decent hatch is taking place I have designed a hatching grey phantom nymph with a transparent body. If this pattern is fished on the dropper with the grey nymph on the point during the hatch and for some time after it, some very exciting fishing can occur, particularly if you are fishing water where there are only wild brown trout. The takes will come from nowhere and a lot will be missed, but it will stir up the adrenalin.

Hatching Grey Phantom Nymph *(Plate 10)*
Tying silk Green
Body Clear PVC
Rib Silver wire
Hackle Olive hen
Wing Grey quill feather
Hook Size 12, 14, wide gape

The body material for the hatching grey nymph can be taken from any clear plastic bag so long as it is thin. Cut into a narrow strip and wind. When the body is completed it should be transparent enough to allow the tyer to see the green silk body underneath. The wing should be narrow and short, no longer than the body. For the wing take a narrow strip of feather from a mallard's grey wing quill; fold it and tie in; if you find you have tied it in too long take the scissors and adjust the length, taking care to keep the pointed end of the wing; the fish will not notice if it has been cut.

Green Nymph
Tying silk Red
Body Insect-green floss
Hackle Olive
Hook Size 12, 14, wide gape

Hatching Green Nymph
Tying silk Red
Body Insect-green floss
Hackle Olive
Wing Grey quill
Hook Size 12, 14, wide gape

The dressing and fishing of them are the same as the phantom nymphs; the only difference is the nice bright red silk head which makes the green nymphs more effective.

The Green and Hatching Green Nymphs are useful patterns at Colliford Lake; in 1988 there were some tremendous hatches of them and the fish became very selective for days. Using the Green Nymph on the point and the Hatching Green Nymph on the dropper I managed to take a few fish in these conditions.

Yellow Nymph
Tying silk   Red
Body   Primrose yellow goose herl
Hackle   Olive
Wing   Grey quill
Hook   Size 12, 14, wide gape

Yellow Hatching Nymph
Tying silk   Red
Body   Primrose yellow goose herl
Hackle   Olive
Wing   Grey quill
Hook   Size 12, 14, wide gape

Dressing and fishing these are the same as the grey and green nymphs. There has been some sizeable hatches of the yellow body species at Colliford, sometimes the same time as the green species. It is very difficult when this happens, particularly when the greys, browns and blacks are on the wing at the same time.

Black Hatching Nymph
Tying silk   Claret
Body   Black herl
Rib   Silver wire
Hackle   Black or dark blue
Wing   Grey quill

The same dressing is used for the **Brown Hatching Nymph** except the body is herl from pheasant centre tail, and grey hackle.

Rabley's March Brown – *Rabley*
Body   Olive-yellow herl
Rib   Silver wire
Hackle   Brown partridge
Wing   Pheasant wing
Hook   Size 12, 14, wide gape

Very good when March brown are about. Fishing this pattern will give good sport; it was at one time very popular on the Cornwall/Devon border in the Launceston area.

Infallible – *Designer unknown*
Tail   Dark blue dun hackle fibres
Tying silk   Claret
Body   Mole fur dubbed – leave some turns of silk at tail end exposed
Hackle   Dark blue dun

Very good fished wet, useful when the iron blues are on the water.

Rusty Red – *Designer unknown*
Tail Rusty blue dun hackle fibres
Body Hare's ear
Rib Gold wire
Hackle Rusty blue cock

An all round pattern representing many natural flies, it is a good pattern when the blue dun is hatching, fished wet. Both Rusty Red and Infallible are at their best if dressed on size 14 size gape hook.

Silver March Brown – *Designer unknown*
Tail Brown partridge fibres
Body Silver tinsel
Rib Oval silver tinsel
Hackle Brown partridge
Wing Hen pheasant wing
Hook Size 8, 10, 12, wide gape

Welsh Patterns

Dogsbody (wet or dry) – *H. Powell*
Tail Pheasant tail fibres
Body Camel coloured dog hair dubbed on brown silk
Hackle Grizzle with natural red hackle in front
Hook Size 12, 14, wide gape

Harry Powell, a well known fly-dresser on the Usk, created the Dogsbody from the hair combing of a local dog. This fly is very popular in Wales. A few combings out of any yellow-brown dog will produce enough material for dozens of flies.

March Brown Spider (Welsh pattern) – *Unknown*
Tail Brown Partridge
Body Dark hare's ear mixed with a little claret seal's fur
Rib Silver oval tinsel
Hackle Long fibre brown partridge
Hook Size 8, 10, 12, 14, wide gape

Coch-y-Bondhu (wet) – *Unknown*
Body Peacock herl
Hackle Furnace
Hook Size 12, 14, wide gape

Very good when this beetle appears in very large swarms in June. In some areas it is known as bracken clock or June Bug, and is very common in some localities in Wales. A useful variation has a gold tinsel tag or gold rib and a pheasant red neck hackle edged with black in place of the furnace hackle. There is no need to buy a furnace cape – use the red-black feathers from the common pheasant. The fly so dressed will probably be most attractive to the trout.

Dark Mackerel – *Unknown*
Tail Pheasant tail fibres
Body Purple seal's fur
Rib Gold wire
Hackle Dark purple
Wing Brown mallard
Hook Size 12, 14, wide gape

The Dark Mackerel is an old dressing that is still popular in Wales and in the borders of Cornwall and Devon in the Launceston area.

It is most useful when the March Browns are about; an early season pattern.

Michael Shephard has popularized the Haul-y-Gwynt in Cornwall and Devon and it is proving effective in taking fish in all sorts of situations, from fishing on sunk lines to being greased up and fished dry. There is a difference of opinion on what the dressing should be: Raymond Jones of Gaerwen insists there is no rib; Wilf Childs ties his version with a fine silver rib. Both anglers are agreed that the dark red-brown hackle edged with black is better than a light-coloured hackle. They also say that a hackle from a melanistic pheasant is very good. Many anglers do not tie in the wing – just a hackle fly. Jim Parry of Gaerwen and some his friends tie a variant with a grey partridge hackle as well as the pheasant hackle and use a red, green or silver tinsel body, without a wing.

Hugh Owen of Llanfechell ties a fly with the wing as per pattern and the usual cock pheasant red-brown hackle, but varies the body materials. He has recently had success with a body dressed with red mohair knitting wool dubbed onto the tying silk. Mr Owen, who is regarded by many as an expert Alaw fly angler, ties a lightly dressed pattern so that it looks as near as possible to an insect.

Haul-y-Gwynt (Sun and Wind) – *Unknown*
Body   Black seal's fur
Wing   Grey feather (sedge style)
Hackle   Red-brown pheasant edged with black
Hook   Size 8, 10, 12

Grannom – *John Jackson*
Tag   Green silk
Body   Hare's ear
Hackle   Grizzle
Wings   Hen pheasant
Hook   Size 10, 12, wide gape

Red Clock – *John Jackson*
Body   Brown peacock herl
Hackle   Red-brown cock pheasant
Head   Bright red tying silk
Hook   Size 10, 12, wide gape

Two good patterns throughout the season on river and lake.

6

The Wet Spiders

Not enough attention has been given by fly-fishers to the very sparsely dressed flies which go under the collective name of spiders. Apparently they are still used quite a lot in the north of the United Kingdom and Michael Shephard, a noted angling writer, tells me the northern dressed spider patterns of today are quite heavily dressed in comparison to the spiders of W. C. Stewart who wrote *The Practical Angler* in 1857.

It would appear Stewart discovered the worth of the sparsely dressed some years previously and in his book he writes, 'For more than fifteen years we have pursued angling with the greatest assiduity; and during that period have obtained information from a number of excellent amateur anglers. We have also fished with, and watched while fishing, almost all the best professional anglers of the day including the celebrated James Baille, considered by all who knew him the ablest flyfisher in Scotland, and from whom we have received some valuable information upon that branch of art.'

Stewart used a twelve foot rod and silk line for flyfishing and practised fishing the fly upstream, which in my view is far the best way. Fishing the spider upstream on a relatively short line enables the angler to present his fly without the fish being disturbed; the fly will move naturally, tumbling and twisting in whichever direction the waterflow takes it; the water will agitate the dressing of the artificial causing the hackle fibres to open and close like the legs of an insect to impart the 'life' to the fly, which will make it attractive to trout.

When fishing the wet fly upstream a long rod makes it easier to keep in touch with your flies and helps to make more effective hooking of fish; very often the only indication of a take is a 'flash' in the water which is caused by the trout taking the fly and turning away; lift the rod tip and it should be hooked. This can be very exciting fishing and with experience you will acquire the timing so that not many trout are missed.

The advantage of fishing the fly upwards on small streams is if you are working your way up and covering every likely-looking piece of water, should you hook a fish it is easy to play it downstream and net it, thus leaving the water upstream still undisturbed. If fishing small streams across and down, usually once a fish has been caught the chances of taking a second one at the same place are remote as the jumping and plunging of the first fish in all directions will have alarmed its neighbours. On the larger rivers this point is not quite so important and plenty of fish can be caught by the down and across method of fishing. This will help the inexperienced angler to acquire the skills to fish the 'fly' before moving onto the upstream method of flyfishing, which will make it possible for him to take trout consistently in little streams like the rivers Inny, Carey and Kensey on the Tamar system, which are useful little trout fisheries.

The correct method of fishing a medium to large river with the wet fly is to cast the fly partly upstream and across from where the angler is standing; allow the fly to fish down for a few yards then lift off and cast again; never allow the fly to go downstream of the angler. When the water has been thoroughly fished, move upstream a few yards and repeat the process.

Stewart stresses in his book that the spiders must be sparsely dressed and the colour in certain conditions is not that important as if a fly is being rolled around by every current and sometimes seen only through a few feet of running water and against the sky, the idea the trout can detect the colour to a shade is highly improbable. I don't know if trout can or cannot see colours distinctly in that sort of situation but it is my experience that different colours does make a difference to trout behaviour. I do not think the exact colour to be that important providing it is reasonably close. Stewart goes on to a point with which I totally agree, that in fly-dressing the object is to make the artificial fly resemble the natural insect in shape, and the great characteristic of all river insects is extreme lightness and neatness of form.

The wet spider has every possible advantage: it is more like the natural aquatic insect; it is lightly dressed and it falls gently on the water, and every flyfisher knows the importance of good presentation.

To dress the spider you need only tying silk and hackles. The hackles are the most important items and I use hackles from a wide range of birds, taking them from the neck and shoulders or the inside of wings from the pheasant, woodcock, partridge, wood pidgeon, coot, moorhen, jackdaw, jay, and farmyard fowls. I do not normally use starling hackles because I consider them too soft; however for the upstream spider patterns they are ideal and one would be a fool not to take advantage of this fact where durability is not important.

Stewart gives his list of hackles as starling, landrail, dotterel, mavis, grey plover, partridge and grouse. He states the selection of proper feathers requires some care: they should be always taken from birds when in their full plumage. Should they not be easily available those considered most necessary are hackles, which are usually taken from the neck of the common farmyard fowl. He complains it is difficult to procure them of the right colour, and still more so to procure them of the right shape. He goes on to state that in a proper hackle the fibres (barbs) should be longest at the root end, and taper gradually towards the point and there is not one cock out of twenty whose hackles merits the attention of the fly-dresser. This specification is totally the opposite of what I consider to be a perfect hackle shape. In Chapter 12 I describe poultry hackle, quality and shape in considerable detail.

When I select a hackle to dress a spider I look for a very soft feather that will impart life to the artificial. A hackle when held by the stalk in a breeze will quiver and the individual fibres ripple around in the air currents. When this hackle is tied into a fly and placed in the water the motion will impart a realistic life-like effect to the spider when fished upstream. If a fly dressed with such a hackle is fished downstream, when the fly is drawn up against the current all life-like motion is suppressed; a spider dresed with a stiffer hackle from a hen would be more suitable for this type of fishing.

To dress the spider, first start tying the silk midway on the hookshank and wind to hookeye with even turns; select the hackle and tie in; wind the hackle one complete turn or one and half turns around hookshank. Secure the hackle, taking the silk back through it and binding down the hackle stalk. Cut off surplus hackle and complete head with whip finish.

There are some anglers who prefer their spiders half palmer style; this does tend to make the spider more heavily dressed as a longer hackle has to be used, in order to do one and half turns. To dress this style, first wind the silk from hookeye to halfway down the hookshank, bring the tying silk back up the shank to about one third of the distance of hookshank from eye. Tie in hackle by the tip and wind the tying silk up through the hackle and secure; cut off surplus hackle and whip finish. Spiders tied with soft hackles are not very durable: the trout's teeth soon tear them to pieces and little is left apart from the bare silk body, so the angler needs to carry a good supply of spiders. I take a lot of my spider hackles from the outside and inside of wings and the underbelly of birds. I am particularly fond of the wood-cock's plumage and the blue-black or blue-green hackles from a melanistic pheas-ant; medium or dark blue hackles I take from the waterhen; the light blue from the woodpigeon or jay.

In his book Stewart gives three dressings of spiders which he considered all that was necessary. In 1987 Michael Shephard wrote an article in the *Trout and Salmon* about Stewart Spiders for which I dressed the flies to provide the illustrations for the article. The dressings as given by Stewart are:

The Black Spider
This is made of the small feather of the cock starling, dressed with brown silk and is, on the whole, the most killing imitation we know.

The Red Spider
Should be made of the small feather taken from the outside of the wing of the landrail, dressed with yellow silk, and is deserving of very high rank, particularly in coloured water.

The Dun Spider
This should be made of the small soft dun or ash-coloured feather taken from the outside of the wing of the dotterel. This bird is unfortunately very scarce, but a small feather may be taken from the inside of the wing of the starling, which will make an excellent substitute.

Stewart also gives his instruction on how to dress the spiders: 'Take the hook between finger and thumb and with a well waxed thread, commencing about the centre of the hook, whip it and the gut firmly together, till you come to end of the shank, where form the head by a few turns of thread. This done, take the feather and laying it on with the root end towards the bend of the hook, wrap the silk three or four times round it, and then cut off root end. Still holding the hook between forefinger and thumb, take the thread, lay it along the centre of the inside of the feather, and with the forefinger and thumb of other hand twirl them round together till the feather is rolled round the thread; and in this state wrap it round the hook, taking care that a sufficient number of the fibres stick out to form the legs; to effect this it will sometimes be necessary to raise the fibres with a needle during the operation. Having carried the feather and thread down to where you commenced, wrap the silk three or four times round end of feather, and if there is any left cut it off, and finish with a succession of hitch-knots, or the common whip-hastening. If the legs of the spider when dressed are too long, there is no remedy for it, cutting injures rather than improves them.'

Stewart found that in the early part of the season before the appearance of the real insects the larger artificials killed well, and he would subscribe to the circumstance that trout will take a larger fly in May than June. That trout will sometimes take more readily flies of one colour than another is certain and the reason for this allows a great deal of speculation. He thinks to some extent certain colours in the right circumstances are more readily seen. In clear water he rarely found a black fly surpassed by any other, and in such circumstances a black fly was very easily seen. In dark water a yellow-bodied fly or one of dingy white colour, takes readily, being easily seen. An angler can always choose the colour of his flies by experience; in practise it has been proved beyond doubt that black, brown, red and dun-coloured fly, used together, and varied in size according to circumstances will take fish.

All this I have found by experience to be true, and accordingly I have designed a range of Spiders which will meet any fishing situation the angler may find himself in. I have divided the spiders into two groups, upstream spiders and across and down-stream spiders. The upstream flies I have designed to be dressed with very soft mobile pulsating flowing hackles. The across and downstream flies are dressed with hen hackles or coarse gamebird hackles. Of course the across and down spiders can be fished upstream and be quite effective, whereas the upstream spiders if fished down in fast water would not give their best.

The upstream dressings are not noted for their durability so dress half a dozen of each type.

Across and Down Spiders

March Brown Spider
Tying silk　Brown
Hackle　Brown partridge

Grey March Brown Spider
Tying Silk　Grey
Hackle　Brown partridge

Two early season patterns that can be used in larger sizes in March and April, then reduce the hook sizes for May and June which is probably the end of season for them.

Black Spider
Tying Silk　Black
Hackle　Black hen

Iron Blue Spider
Tying Silk　Red
Hackle　Water hen

Brown Spider
Tying silk　Brown
Hackle　Woodcock

These three patterns will come into season mid or late April and be useful right throughout the fishing season.

Yellow Spider
Tying Silk　Yellow
Hackle　Woodcock

Orange Spider
Tying silk   Orange
Hackle   Woodcock

Olive Spider
Tying silk   Olive
Hackle   Dark olive hen

These three patterns are useful from May onwards

Upstream Spiders

The colour combinations are endless; the dressings I have given are all proven designs and have taken their share of fish in all hook sizes. I will leave it to the tyer to decide what size hooks to dress his spiders on. I usually use size 10, 12, 14, wide gape; for the early season March browns I will step up to size 8, wide gape.

Grey Spider – Upstream
Tying silk   Grey
Hackle   Grey partridge. Select very pale hackle from underneath partridge belly – must be soft and fluffy.

Black Spider – Upstream
Tying silk   Black
Hackle   Jackdaw or starling

Iron Blue Spider – Upstream
Tying silk   Red
Hackle   Jackdaw or starling – select light coloured hackle from head of jackdaw or inside wing of starling

Yellow Spider – Upstream
Tying silk   Yellow
Hackle   Woodcock or quail

The quail is the softer hackle, but if not available there are plenty of soft fluffy hackles on woodcock, usually under the tail area or underwings.

Orange Spider – Upstream
Tying silk   Orange
Hackle   Woodcock or quail

Three spider dressing I have designed for low water sea trout fishing during the day are included in the sea trout pattern list. They are just as effective for any other sort of fish.

7

Sea Trout Flies

The rivers Fowey and Camel are small spate rivers which have a good run of sea trout. It was whilst fishing these rivers I learned the skills to catch sea trout, developing at the same time the sea trout flies.

Both these rivers have their source on Bodmin Moor in the shadows of the only two mountains in Cornwall. The river Camel starts its life north of Camelford and meanders over the moor, down through wooded valleys and on past green fields until it reaches the tidal stretch at the town of Wadebridge, a distance of some twenty-five miles from where it bubbles up out of the ground. North of Bolventor, the river Fowey starts its journey to the sea; flowing over twenty miles, passing through moorland then fields and wild wooded valleys, it meets the salt water in the tidal reaches at Lostwithiel.

Sea trout start running both rivers in late April, usually the large sea trout at first run in singly or in twos and threes, followed by the school peal in July. Most seasons there are very small numbers of sea trout running all summer. There can also be a sizeable run at the end of the season, from late September to early November, which is often called the harvest peal.

The river Tamar is the natural boundary between Cornwall and Devon. In the Tamar system, the sea trout normally arrive in the Launceston area about mid-July. Most years the bulk of the run seems to be attracted to the main tributary of the Tamar – the river Lyd. If there should be a good level of water, the Inny, another but smaller tributary of the Tamar which is downstream of the Lyd, will have a reasonable run of sea trout; however if the water is low there is not enough depth to encourage them to turn and come over the shallows at Inny foot and they will carry on up the Tamar which ensures the Lyd has a good run of sea trout for that year.

Although sea trout can be taken on fly during the day using the correct method, the normal practice in Devon and Cornwall is to start fishing at dusk, as soon as the bats appear on the wing. I like to start as a rule with a Jungle Alexander on; if after a half hour or so it has produced no result I change to a dark fly like Mallard and Claret, Teal and Blue, Zula or the Keeper patterns. It is my experience that flies dressed with very slim wings are usually the most effective; with fresh run sea trout the longer the fly the better is its killing power. Normally the fish do not hang about if there is plenty of water; with low water conditions the situation will change and the fish will move up river very slowly, becoming stale and difficult to tempt. This is the time that small flies become very effective and good catches can be had.

The dressings that follows are patterns that I have developed for sea trout over the years. Some of them are also very effective in raising lake trout, particularly the rainbow trout. It has been known even for the occasional salmon to make a mistake and grab them.

Depth Charge *(Plate 11)*
Tail   Golden pheasant tippet
Body   First silver tinsel, followed by D.F.M. orange wool, ribbed silver oval
Hackle   Furnace
Wing   Brown mallard shoulder dressed slim
Hook   Size 6, 8, 10, wide gape

Keeper Series

David Clarke, Head Gamekeeper of Boconnoc Estate, Lostwithiel, is partly responsible for the success of the Keeper Series flies and the names I have given them. Five years ago I first tied a batch of flies for him and his friends to use whilst fishing for sea trout on the river Fowey. I also gave him some experimental tyings to test; from his and other test results the following Keeper series of flies evolved. So effective were they he keeps coming back each year for more.

The Keeper *(Plate 11)*
Tail   Feather slip from goose shoulder, dyed bright red
Body   Bright yellow wool or seal's fur, ribbed gold oval
Wing   Cock pheasant green rump dressed killer style
Hackle   Green rump
Hook   Size 6, 8, longshank

Underkeeper
Tail   Dyed red goose
Body   Silver tinsel, ribbed oval
Wing   Cock pheasant green rump dressed killer style
Hackle   Green rump
Cheeks   Jungle cock or substitute
Hook   Size 6, 8, longshank

Beatkeeper
Tail   Dyed blue goose
Body   Red wool or seal's fur, ribbed silver oval
Wing   Cock pheasant green rump dressed killer style
Sides   Dyed blue goose
Hackle   Green rump
Hook   Size 6, 8, longshank

Headkeeper
Tail   Dyed red goose
Body   Peacock herl
Wing   Melanistic cock pheasant rump
Hackle   Blue green rump
Cheeks   Jungle cock or substitute
Hook   Size 6, 8, longshank

For the Keeper and Underkeeper dyed red feather slips from a goose shoulder can be added on the sides; this at times appears to make the flies more effective.

Killer style wings require whole feathers; each fly can have two or four feathers, it is the tyer's choice. The easy way for tying in whole feather wings is to strip the feather to the required size, tie in the feather by its stalk on the side of the hook with a couple turns of silk, catch hold of the stalk and pull it towards the eye. When the leading fibres of the feather start going under the silk, stop – you will find this causes the feather to veil the body better as it makes a more streamlined fly in the water. When tying in the green rump for the hackle, tie it in close to the eye, wind it as a collar and sweep the fibres back over the wing and body and overtie. This helps to make a very streamlined fly while being fished.

Lady Gwen *(Plate 11)*
Tail   Dyed red duck feather slip
Body   White ostrich herl, ribbed silver oval
Hackle   White hen
Wing   Grey mallard
Hook   Size 6, 8, wide gape

Lord Penpont *(Plate 11)*
Tail   Dyed yellow duck feather slip
Body   Dyed yellow ostrich herl, ribbed gold oval
Hackle   Light cree cock
Wing   Grey mallard
Hock   Size 6, 8, wide gape

Lady Inny *(Plate 11)*
Tail   Dyed orange duck feather slip
Body   Orange ostrich herl
Wing   Grey mallard
Hackle   Golden pheasant tippet wound as collar
Hook   Size 6, 8, 10, 12, wide gape

Lady Luck *(Plate 11)*
Tail   Dyed red duck feather slip
Body   Silver tinsel with dyed blue ostrich over ribbed silver oval
Hackle   Blue peacock neck feather
Wing   Brown mallard shoulder
Cheeks   Jungle cock
Hook   Size 6, 8, wide gape

Teal and Black *(Plate 11)*
Tail   Blue peacock feather fibres
Body   Black seal's fur, ribbed silver oval
Hackle   Blue-black pheasant feather
Wing   Teal flank dressed slim
Hook   Size 6, 8, 10, wide gape

Teal and Purple
Tail   Blue peacock feather fibres
Body   Purple seal's fur, ribbed silver oval
Hackle   Blue peacock feather
Wing   Teal flank dressed slim
Hook   Size 6, 8, 10, wide gape

Teal and Orange *(Plate 11)*
Tail   Golden pheasant tippet
Body   Orange seal's fur, ribbed gold oval
Hackle   Golden pheasant tippet
Wing   Teal flank dressed slim
Hook   Size 6, 8, 10, wide gape

Some tyers experience difficulty in handling teal, mallard flank and mallard brown shoulders for winging. The art of good teal and mallard wings is in the preparation of the feathers before tying in.

For the mallard shoulders and flank feathers: take two narrow slips from the side of feather; ensuring there is not too much natural curve to the feather slips, place one on top of other. Carefully line the feather tips straight; when satisfied they are in line, fold them and tie them in. This technique will work with the better class teal flank feathers, but for the majority of small teal feathers the following technique is useful.

Prepare your feather by stripping off the surplus fibres up the stalk until you reach the fibres you wish to tie in. With the scissors, select the width you require and cut off stalk. You are now left holding a stalk with two slips of feather each side; these slips are the width you have already selected for the wing. Moisten the fibres so that they will hold together, fold them to form the wing and then tie them in. Cut off stalk and surplus feather. This technique will give a passable wing from a small teal feather which a lot of tyers cannot be bothered to prepare and use.

Peacock Fly *(Plate 11)*
Tail   Red goose feather slip
Body   Silver tinsel, ribbed silver oval
Wing   Peacock blue neck killer style
Cheeks   Jungle cock
Hackle   Blue peacock dressed as collar
Hook   Longshank or two hook tandem

Peacock Red Tag
Tail   Red wool
Body   Peacock herl
Hackle   Blue or green peacock

The Peacock Red Tag is effective in any size from size twelve wide gape up to size two longshank, using peacock green hackle for the small sizes and blue hackle for the larger dressing. It is a very versatile pattern and it has taken the full range of game fish.

Alexandra – *(Standard pattern)*
Tail   Red ibis
Body   Silver tinsel, ribbed silver oval
Hackle   Black
Wing   Peacock sword feather
Sides   Red ibis

The Alexandra I originally found to be one of the most effective sea trout patterns but I have since devised variations that on Cornish waters have proved to be even more effective, in fact quite deadly.

Red Alexandra
Tail   Red ibis
Body   Silver tinsel, ribbed silver oval
Hackle   Peacock blue neck
Wing   Peacock sword
Sides   Red ibis
Head   Bright red silk

Blue Alexandra
Same dressing except dyed blue goose shoulders for sides and tail.

Yellow Alexandra
Same dressing except dyed yellow goose for sides and tail.

Jungle Red Alexandra
Same as Red Alexandra except jungle cock eye hackle for cheeks.

Instead of using feather slips for the sides in the Alexandra there is a very mobile plastic tinsel material called Flashabou which is available in various colours. This material when mixed with the sword feather makes the fly take on a glitter which has proved very effective. The most useful hook size for the Alexandra range is size six or eight wide gape. I mostly tied my Alexandra's with the flying treble, thus creating a long winged slim-looking fly.

Blue Mackerel
Tail   Blue peacock neck
Body   Silver tinsel, ribbed silver oval
Body hackle   White cock
Hackle   Blue peacock
Wing   Dyed blue teal flank
Hook   Size 6, 8, longshank

Yellow Fly *(Plate 11)*
Tail   Two small tippets back to back (to give a fish shape)
Body   Gold tinsel, ribbed gold oval
Body hackle   Dyed yellow cock
Hackle   Golden pheasant rump
Wing   Dyed yellow grey mallard flank
Hook   Size 6, 8, longshank

Green Minnow *(Plate 11)*
Tail   Two small tippets back to back
Body   Copper tinsel, ribbed copper wire
Body hackle   Cree cock
Hackle   Cock pheasant green rump feather
Wing   Peacock sword
Hook   Size 6, 8, longshank

Ramsbottom's Favourite – *R. Ramsbottom* – *(Plate 11)*
Tail   Red ibis
Body   Yellow seal's fur ribbed gold oval
Hackle   Coch-y-bondhu
Wing   Married red-yellow-blue duck or goose shoulders, golden pheasant tail, brown mallard
Hook   Size 6, 8, wide gape

It is recommended before fishing with this fly that you run a needle through the wing, thereby breaking the married wing which will impart more life to the fly. The married wing is after all just a technique to prepare various colours of feather slips to enable the tyer to tie them all in together – thus reducing number of silk turns which helps to keep the fly head small and neat *(see page 90)*.

Freeman's Fancy – *W. Freeman* – *(Plate 11)*
Tail   Toucan or topping
Body   Gold tinsel, ribbed gold oval
Body hackle   Magenta cock
Hackle   Claret hen

Wing   Brown mallard
Hook   Size 6, 8, 10, 12 wide gape

A very effective sea trout fly, also very good for lake trout in the smaller sizes – the rainbow trout will sometimes really chop it. Jungle cheeks can be added in the larger sizes.

Mallard and Claret – *W. Murdoch (Plates 1–4)*
Tail   Golden pheasant tippet
Body   Claret seal's fur, ribbed gold oval
Hackle   Black cock
Wing   Brown mallard
Hook   Size 6, 8, 10, 12, wide gape

A splendid pattern for river or lake, no flyfisher should be without a dressing of this fly in his box.

Red Mallard and Claret *(Plate 11)*
Tail   Tippet
Body   Dark claret seal's fur, ribbed size 16 gold oval tinsel
Hackle   Woodcock
Wing   Brown mallard
Head   Bright red silk clear varnished
Hook   Size 6, 8, 10, 12, wide gape

Although this is a variation of Murdoch's fly I designed it for sea trout in an attempt to improve on the standard dressing; this I think I have done – the sea trout takes it well. Chris Martindale fished it at Colliford Lake where on several occasions he really got into the wild brown trout. It appears it is a good all-rounder and a pattern that should be always available in the fly box.

Coachman – *T. Bosworth* – *(Plate 11)*
Body   Peacock herl
Hackle   Red game
Wing   White duck quill
Hook   8, 10, 12, 14, wide gape

A useful pattern – fishing a size ten wide gape hook with a slim wing coachman dressing, I caught four sea trout one afternoon in the river Inny. I think the sea trout took it for a moth. Fishing the river Camel at Dunmere thirty years ago, I took fourteen sea trout in an evening fishing on the Coachman. A friend fishing with me also had ten fish on the same pattern.

Heckham and Peckham – *W. Murdoch* – *(Plate 11)*
Tail   Red cock fibres, silver tag
Body   Hare's ear
Hackle   Red game
Wing   White tipped mallard blue quill
Hook   6, 8, 10, wide gape

Butcher – *Standard pattern*
Tail   Red ibis
Body   Silver tinsel, ribbed silver oval
Hackle   Black cock
Wing   Mallard blue quill
Hook   6, 8, 10, wide gape

Zulu – *Standard pattern*
Tag   Red wool
Body   Black seal's fur, ribbed size 16 oval tinsel
Body Hackle   Black cock
Hackle   Black cock

Blue Zulu – *Standard pattern*
Tag   Red wool
Body   Black seal's fur, ribbed oval silver tinsel
Body hackle   Black cock
Hackle   Blue cock

The two hook lures have been designed for fishing sea trout during the day with fast sinking lines on short leaders in deep runs and pools. This style of fishing can be very productive, particularly if there is a tinge of colour in the water. The sea trout will usually take the fly as the line curves across the current and speeds the lure up.

In the deep slow pools it will be necessary to strip the line quickly to make the lure work properly and there is always a chance of a salmon using this technique. It is important that the lures should be not less than 5 cm (2 in) long; fresh run sea trout in the lower reaches will really chop them.

Silver Grey Lure *(Plate 12)*
Hooks   Size 6, wide gape front and rear
Tail   D.F.M. orange wool
Body   Silver tinsel, ribbed silver oval
Hackle   Long-fibred golden pheasant red breast
Wing   Grey mallard flank
Cheeks   Jungle cock or substitute

Silver Blue Lure *(Plate 12)*
Hooks   Size 6, wide gape front and rear
Tail   Red wool
Body   Silver tinsel, ribbed silver oval
Hackle   Long fibred blue peacock
Wing   Grey mallard flank dyed blue
Cheeks   Jungle cock or substitute

Claret and Mallard *(Plate 12)*
Hooks   Size 6, wide gape front and rear
Tail   Magenta wool
Body   Dark claret seal's fur, ribbed gold oval tinsel
Hackle   Golden pheasant red breast
Wing   Brown mallard

Silver Ghost Lure *(Plate 12)*
Hooks   Size 6, wide gape front and rear
Tail   White D.F.M. wool
Body   SIlver tinsel, ribbed oval
Hackle   White cock
Wing   Grey mallard flank
Cheeks   Red wool clipped short

Alexandra Lure *(Plate 12)*
Hooks   Size 6, 8, wide gape front and rear
Tail   Dyed red goose

Body   Silver tinsel, ribbed oval
Hackle   Blue peacock
Wing   Peacock sword
Sides   Dyed red goose
Cheeks   Jungle cock or substitute

Dunkeld Lure *(Plate 12)*
Hook   Size 6, 8, wide gape front and rear
Tail   Yellow D.F.M. wool
Body   Gold tinsel, ribbed oval
Hackle   Hot orange cock
Wing   Brown mallard
Cheeks   Jungle cock or substitute

Butcher Lure *(Plate 12)*
Hook   Size 6, 8, wide gape front and rear
Tail   Red wool
Body   Silver ribbed, oval tinsel
Hackle   Dyed red cock
Wing   Black squirrel

Dirty Water Lure *(Plate 12)*
Hook   Size 6, wide gape front and rear
Tail   Hot orange cock fibres
Body   Red wool ribbed silver oval tinsel
Hackle   Hot orange cock
Wing   Red-blue-silver Flashabou mixed

Red Flashabou Tube *(Plate 12)*
Body   Silver tinsel
Wing   Red Flashabou

Blue Flashabou Tube *(Plate 12)*
Body   Silver tinsel
Wing   Blue Flashabou

The uses for Flashabou and other plastic tinsel material in fly-tying is endless, and I expect the use of these and other new materials to increase as time goes on because of their availability and the shortage of traditional materials.

When weather conditions are suitable during the summer days it is possible to take sea trout during daylight hours by using fine leaders and small flies in low water. If the day is hot with the sun blazing down, to go sea trout fishing will be largely a waste of time.

If the sky should cloud over and become overcast, this is the time you are in with a chance. Fish the runs or any place where the flow of current oxygenates the water, under overhead vegetation, under the banks, anywhere the fish could have taken cover. At the head of pools where the fast water in the shallows above has been agitated by the rocky river bed causing bubbles thus oxygenating the water, the fish will lie taking what oxygen they can. For low water conditions during the day, taking advantage of any cloudy overcast that may occur, I have designed the following flies.

Low Water Spiders

Black L.W. Spider
Body　Strand of black floss, ribbed silver wire
Hackle　Blue-black from cock pheasant neck

Black/Orange L.W. Spider
Body　Strand of D.F.M. orange wool
Hackle　Blue-black from cock pheasant neck

Black/Green L.W. Spider
Body　Strand of D.F.M. lime green wool
Hackle　Blue-black from cock pheasant neck

The hook size for the low water spiders is a wide gape size twelve; they can be dressed on a size fourteen but there would be no point going any smaller. It is important the spiders are lightly dressed. The wool bodies should consist of only one strand which has been unravelled from the main length of wool. The hackle is from the common pheasant neck, one turn only around hookshank and the fibres no longer than the hook gape. The body should be no longer than three-quarters of the hookshank. In all, a very light sparsely dressed fly if the fish are to be induced. Don't forget the fine leaders – you will have to take a chance of it being broken. Using these flies with the correct tactics it is possible to put a couple of fish in the creel while the other fishing guests at the hotel are waiting for evening so they can move onto the bankside and prepare for night fishing.

The next three flies are suitable for daytime fishing for sea trout and trout; they can be useful for sea trout when the water is low. These flies are palmer hackled with very lightly dressed seal fur bodies. Dress the palmers on size ten or twelve mayfly hooks; they can be fished wet or dry.

Claret Palmer
Tail　Pheasant centre tail fibres
Body　Claret seal's fur, ribbed gold wire
Body hackle　Red game cock
Hackle　Red game

Yellow Palmer
Tail　Pheasant tail fibres
Body　Yellow seal's fur, ribbed gold wire
Body hackle　Red game
Hackle　Red game

Orange Palmer
Tail　Pheasant tail fibres
Body　Orange seal's fur, ribbed gold wire
Body hackle　Red game
Hackle　Red game

Low water conditions probably presents the fly fisherman with the most difficult fishing for sea trout or salmon, particularly during daylight hours. The golden rule for any mode of fishing is to keep out of sight. For daytime low water sea trout fishing, if you don't keep out of sight, you don't put anything in the creel. No matter how well the angler is equipped, infallible flies or anything else, letting the fish see you means you don't see them. To be successful means starting at the downstream end of the beat and fishing upstream, taking advantage of every piece of cover on the bank. If the water is large enough to wade, make sure you have cover behind so you are not silhouetted against a light-coloured background. Although studded waders are right for normal fishing practice as they give you a more secure footing, they tend to grate and clatter every time you move and for low water fishing that helps to keep the bag empty. Rubber soles are better, but you could slip and fall and you must weigh up carefully the risks involved against the pleasures of a full bag.

I cannot emphasize enough the importance of concealment, if you wish to be successful. Often I have slowly and carefully approached from downstream a shoal of sea trout lying at the bottom end of a pool, thinking I have not been seen, then all at once the fish will move across to the other bank or upstream. Sometimes they will leave the pool and go downstream and it may take hours before they will come back again. Sea trout fishing in Cornwall and Devon on small rivers in low water conditions during the day can be the most difficult frustrating fly-fishing possible; it sorts the men out from the boys, very often I am just a lad.

8

Lures

The fly lure in the last forty years has become an important addition to the fly-fisher's repertoire for trout on still waters. The increase in reservoirs which have been created and opened for fly-fishing has brought many more people eager to learn fly-fishing into the sport. This in turn gives people like myself the opportunity to dress flies professionally and sell the results of our labours.

Over the years I have devised many hundreds of patterns of lures, so I have only included in my list the more successful dressings. Most of the patterns are my originals but I am including the more effective lures devised by other tyers.

It was, I think, in 1966 or 1967 that a new fly called the Muddler Minnow came over the Atlantic from North America. This pattern with its unusual deer hair head proved to be remarkably effective and soon became well known, the nearest to a magic fly since the Tups Indispensable. Since its introduction I have devised many patterns with deer hair in the dressing using the spinning technique of tying. With these patterns I have caught fish in all types of waters ranging from bass and mackerel in salt water to trout, salmon and coarse fish in fresh water.

Muddler Minnow – *D. Gapen*
Tail   Feather slip from oak turkey quill
Body   Gold tinsel, ribbed gold oval tinsel
Wing   Grey squirrel flanked each side with slips of oak turkey quill feather
Head   Deer hair spun and clipped to tadpole head shape, leaving the long guard hairs underside of hook to form hackle
Hook   Any size

To dress the Muddler Minnow, tie in the tail feather slip then dress the tinsel body, making sure you leave enough bare hook shank at the head for spinning the deer hair. Tie in the squirrel hairwing using the hair from a grey squirrel tail; coat the silk and hair where tied in with varnish; secure with a two turn whip finish. Now tie in the oak turkey each side of hairwing; trim off surplus hair and feather and whip finish; varnish the whipping and coat the bare hook also. Now spin on the deer hair using the same technique as described for the sedge flies bodies (page 33).

Yellow Trevadlock Killer (*Plate 13*)
Tail   Brown squirrel tail hair
Body   Goldfingering gold floss
Wing   Four teal flank feathers dyed yellow, dressed killer style
Head   Spun deer hair or brown chenille
Hook   Size 6 or 8 longshank

Tea Boy (*Plate 13*)
Tail   Golden pheasant tail fibres
Body   Gold tinsel, ribbed gold oval
Wing   Grey mallard flank dyed brown

Head Spun deer hair clipped
Hook Any size

The grey mallard flanks are first washed to remove the natural grease in the feather and then dyed by putting them in a pan of water with tea leaves and heating. When dyed, the colour of the feather is a somewhat pinkish-brown; it is a very difficult colour to describe so give it a try and see for yourself. The deer hair should be clipped tight but leaving a few hairs underneath to form a hackle. This pattern can be fished deep or on the surface. I used it in a competition at Siblyback Lake and won a large bottle of whisky for the heaviest bag, which speaks for itself.

Orange Marabou Muddler (*Plate 13*)
Body Gold tinsel ribbed gold wire
Wing Orange marabou fibres
Head Dyed orange deer hair clipped
Hook Any size

This dressing is very effective when fished on a floating line in the small sizes during the evening rise. I have known rainbow trout to come after it from yards away, creating a bow wave rather like a submarine coming to the surface at speed.

White Muddler
Body D.F.M. white wool, ribbed gold oval
Wing White calf tail hair
Neck Red wool
Head White deer hair clipped
Hook Any size

Fishing at Crowdy Marsh with this fly dressed on a size twelve longshank hook one evening, a giant of a fish rose and took it on the surface just after it landed after a cast. I played this fish for two or three minutes before it took me into the lake's bottom and smashed me up.

Michael's Muddler
Tag D.F.M. scarlet wool
Body Peacock herl
Wing Grey squirrel tail dyed hot orange flanked with oak turkey strips
Head Deer hair clipped
Hook Any size

Orange Muddler
Tail Dyed red cock fibres
Body Orange wool ribbed silver oval
Wing Grey squirrel dyed hot orange
Head Deer hair dyed hot orange

Yellow Muddler
Tail Dyed yellow cock fibres
Body Yellow wool ribbed silver oval
Wing Calf tail dyed yellow
Head Deer hair dyed yellow

The next three lures are Muddler Streamers which I designed in 1970 for Siblyback Lake. Since then they have proved their worth in water all over the United Kingdom and elsewhere. They are most useful when there are fry around the lake's edge and can be fished on floating or sinking lines.

Siblyback Streamer
Body　Gold tinsel gold wire
Throat Hackle　Dyed yellow cock fibres
Wing　Two cree hackles dyed golden yellow with two grizzle hackles outside, two-thirds
the size of the cree hackles
Neck　D.F.M. scarlet wool
Head　Spun deer hair clipped tadpole shape

The throat hackle for this pattern is tied as a false hackle, not wound. Tie it in long
with the fibres veiling the gold body right back to the hook bend. The wool for the
neck should be tied in after the hackle wing is completed, rather like a woollen
head in front of the wing; then spin the deer hair. The most durable way to tie in
hackle wings is to line the hackles up together and tie them all in at one go. Lay the
hackles on top of the hook with the hackle points pointing out over the space in
front of the hookeye and tie in securely. The wing will now be tied in looking the
wrong way; now trim off the hackle stalks and double the wing back so that it is on
top of the body; overtie and secure. A hackle wing dressed by this method will
never pull out with normal use; after considerable use the hackle stalks may break
but probably by that time the fly will need replacing in any case. To tie in the wool
neck after wing is completed, tie the wool in front of wing and wind over the
doubled-back hackle stalks this method makes a good bulky head of the wing,
then spin on the deer hair.

Black Siblyback Streamer
Body　Silver tinsel, ribbed oval silver
Throat　Black cock fibres
Wing　Two black cock hackles with two grizzle hackles outside, two-thirds the size of the
black hackles
Neck　D.F.M. scarlet wool

Orange Siblyback Streamer
Body　Gold tinsel, ribbed oval gold
Throat　Dyed orange cock fibres
Wing　Dyed orange cock hackles with two grizzle hackles outside, two-thirds the size of
the orange hackles
Neck　D.F.M. scarlet wool

Both the Black and Orange Streamer have deer hair heads that must be tightly
spun and clipped to a neat tadpole shape. There must be no long guard hair left as a
hackle, the head must be clipped so that the D.F.M wool neck can be just seen,
rather like the red flash of real gill covers on fish. All three streamers are most
effective when dressed on size 4 or 6 longshank hooks. On the smaller sizes they
do not work so well and are rather tiresome to tie.

Game Bird Muddlers

The next muddler dressings I call my game bird series; the name becomes apparent
from the materials used for the dressings. I designed them to be a good general
representation of the larger forms of aquatic life ranging from the dragonfly,
damselfly and mayfly nymphs, freshwater shrimp, corixa and various sedge fly
nymphs.

　Make sure, when spinning deer hair on the game bird series, that when first
spinning at the wing's root you place the hair on the hookshank with the tips (the

natural tips, not the cut end) looking towards the tail. If you have made sure there is only a very short length of the cut end of the bunch of deer hair on the hookeye side of your silk, when you pull the silk tight – thus spinning the deer hair – it will envelope the body of the muddler like a hackle that has been wound, swept back and overtied. If this has been done correctly the short cut end of the deer hair will not need any trimming. On the next batches of hair spun, place them on the hookshank in the normal manner. When spinning is completed trim the head in the normal manner being careful to leave the first spinning of guard hairs. The game bird muddlers can be fished on floating or sinking line. I have had most of my success fishing them on a sinktip from the bank, trying to fish them just off the bottom of the lake.

Pheasant Muddler (*Plate 13*)
Tail Fibres from cock pheasant tail
Body Cream wool or seal's fur
Wing Fibres from cock pheasant tail flanked by two reddish feathers edged with black from cock pheasant, neck, dressed killer style
Head Spun deer hair
Hook Size 12, 10, longshank

Green Pheasant Muddler (*Plate 13*)
Tail Fibres from green rump feather
Body Green wool or seal's fur
Wing Fibres from cock pheasant green rump feather flanked by two green rump feathers, dressed killer style
Head Spun deer hair
Hook Size 12, 10, longshank

Golden Pheasant Muddler (*Plate 13*)
Tail Golden pheasant tail feather fibres
Body Gold tinsel ribbed gold wire
Wing Red breast feathers flanked by yellow rump feathers from cock golden pheasant, dressed killer style
Head Spun deer hair
Hook Size 10, 8, longshank

Brown Partridge Muddler (*Plate 13*)
Tail Grey partridge hackle fibres
Body Claret wool or seal's fur
Wing Brown partridge hackles, dressed killer style
Head Dyed brown deer hair
Hook Size 12, 10, 8, Longshank

Grey Partridge Muddler (*Plate 13*)
Tail Hackle fibres
Body Green wool or seal's fur
Wing Grey partridge hackles, dressed killer style
Head Spun deer hair
Hook Size 12, 10, 8, longshank

Yellow Partridge Muddler (*Plate 13*)
Tail Dyed yellow hackle fibres
Body Gold tinsel ribbed gold wire
Wing Grey partridge hackles dyed yellow, dressed killer style

Head Spun deer hair coloured with yellow marking felt pen
Hook Size 12, 10, 8, longshank

Woodcock Muddler (*Plate 13*)
Tail Woodcock feather slip from quill
Body Amber wool or seal's fur
Wing Woodcock hackles, dressed killer style
Head Dyed brown deer hair
Hook Size 12, 10, longshank

Streamer Lures

Streamer lures are a firm favourite when imitating fish fry and the dressings I list have proved effective in both lake and river.

Silver-Black Rock Streamer
Body Silver tinsel, ribbed oval silver
Wing Two black cock hackles with two grizzle hackles outside
Hackle Dyed red cock

Black Rock Streamer (*Plate 14*)
Body D.F.M. scarlet, ribbed oval silver
Wing Two black cock hackles with two grizzle hackles outside
Hackle Dyed red cock

Golden Cree Streamer (*Plate 14*)
Body Gold tinsel, ribbed oval gold
Wing Four cree cock hackles dyed golden yellow
Hackle Dyed yellow cree cock

This pattern is most useful when there is small fry in the margins; cast it out and strip it back fast.

The Silver and Black Rock Streamers will also work quite well when the fry are in the margins; however they will take fish well when used on a sunk line even on cold wintry days when there is no sign of fish on the surface. They can be dressed on any size hook although I prefer size six longshank.

Ron's Streamer (*Plate 14*)
Tail Dyed yellow cock hackle fibres
Body D.F.M. scarlet wool, ribbed silver oval
Wing Four black cock hackles
Hackle Dyed yellow cock

Grizzle and White Streamer
Tail White cock hackle fibres
Body D.F.M. white wool, ribbed gold oval
Wing Two grizzle hackles
Hackle White cock

Yellow Barred Rock Streamer (*Plate 14*)
Tail Brown cock hackle fibres
Body Gold tinsel, ribbed gold oval
Wings Two grizzle hackles dyed yellow
Hackle Red game dressed as collar

Green Barred Rock Streamer
Tail Brown cock hackle fibres

Plate 13: Killer Wing Lures (see Chapter 8)

Tea Boy	Yellow Trevadlock Killer
Trevadlock Killer	D.F.M. Scarlet Killer
D.F.M. Partridge Killer	Pheasant Muddler

| Green Pheasant Muddler | Woodcock Muddler | Grey Partridge Muddler |
| Brown Partridge Muddler | Yellow Partridge Muddler | Golden Pheasant Muddler |

| Orange Marabou Muddler | | Elver Eel |

Plate 14: Streamers (see Chapter 8)

Black Rock
Michael's Streamer
Orange Badger
Grey Ghost
Chief Needabeh
Parmachene Belle

Golden Cree
Yellow Barred Rock
Ron's Streamer
Brown Ghost
Black Ghost
Royal Coachman

Plate 15: Hair Wing and Marabou Trout Lures (see Chapter 8)

Yellowbelly Lure
Grey Squirrel Lure
D.F.M. Black and Green Lure
Black and Orange Marabou Lure
Crowdy Marsh Marabou Lure

Black Chenille Lure
D.F.M. Black Lure
Sweeny Todd
Black Marabou and Peacock Lure
Black Marabou Lure

Plate 16: Salmon Feathered Winged Flies (see Chapter 9)

Silver Doctor
White Doctor
Chalmers
Thunder and Lightning
Orange Parson

Dixon
Torrish
Badger
Canary
Dennison

Childers
Silver Grey
Akroyd
Dunkeld
Avon Eagle

Body   Silver tinsel, ribbed silver oval
Wing   Two grizzle hackles dyed green highlander
Hackle   Red game dressed as collar

Black Streamer (*Plates 5–8*)
Tail   Black cock hackle fibres
Body   Black wool, rib gold oval tinsel
Hackle   Black cock
Wing   Four black cock hackles

Black Chenille Streamer
Tail   Black cock hackle fibres
Body   Black chenille
Hackle   Black cock dressed false
Wing   Four black cock hackles

D.F.M. Whisky Streamer Tandem
Tag   D.F.M. scarlet wool
Body   Gold tinsel ribbed gold wire
Wing   Four cock hackles dyed hot orange
Hackle   Orange cock
Front hook   Size ten longshank
Rear hook   Size ten wide gape

Michael's Streamer (*Plate 14*)
Body   Black wool or seal's fur, ribbed wide silver oval size 17
Hackle   Dressed false-dyed yellow cock hackle fibres with dyed red cock fibres over
Cheeks   Jungle cock or substitute
Wing   Four black cock hackles

This lure can be fished either on the surface or deep. It will work just as well without the jungle cock cheeks, but I for one feel the jungle cock eyes make the fly more attractive to fish. The best way to tie in jungle cock eye feathers with hackle wings is to line them up with the hackle wings and tie them all in together, with eyes and hackle tips pointing out over hookeye. Cut off hackle and jungle cock eye stalks, and then double the whole lot back over the fly body and overtie.

Tying the jungle cock eye stalks in together with the hackle stalks tends to make the head of the lure bigger, but the durability factor outweighs this. Also, using a large size oval tinsel for the rib rather than a flat tinsel improves the quality of the fly and its durability.

The Michael's Streamer has for me lured more fish into my landing net than any other streamer, and the number of fish over three pounds in weight runs well into double figures.

Looking back through my sporting notes brings to mind a typical outing on 12 August 1976 when, taking my son Barry with me, I went out to Siblyback Lake for an evening's fishing. It was quite a windy evening, very hot, and the drought we were suffering made the landscape very burnt, giving a barren look to the grass fields surrounding the lake. The water level was the lowest I had ever seen it since the valley was flooded, probably the lake was only about half full or less.

The sun began to set, the wind dropped a little and a few fish were moving here and there. It was now time to make a start. Tying a size ten wide gape Black & Peacock on the point and a size fourteen D.F.M. Orange Spider on the dropper, I cast a line out. I fished away for half an hour with no results, so I decided to change the point fly; I tied on a Michael's Streamer dressed on a size twelve longshank hook. This appeared to be the answer, because after a few minutes I had a savage take and hooked a large fish, which jumped clear out of the water when feeling the barb. I played the fish and after a considerable battle drew it into the shallows where Barry was waiting to net it. It was big cock rainbow which weighed out just over five pounds – a nice start to the evening's fishing.

Moving around a shore line which is normally covered with water, means watching carefully where you are walking. In places the mud bottom is covered with a thin layer of gravel, which looks okay until you step on it, as I found out to my cost. In one place I sank nearly down to the top of my waders and it was a good job Barry was there to help me out – that experience did not do the heart condition any favours. Fishing on, sport was quite slow but I managed to catch two small rainbows which made it a memorable evening, particularly as it had not been a good fishing year.

It was in June 1977 just before I went to Brompton Hospital, London, for open heart surgery that I caught seven trout on a Michael's Streamer that weighed a total of 24³/₄ lb. The catch were all rainbow trout and the excitement coupled with the physical stress of catching and landing brought on a touch of angina which made me rest between catching and landing the last three fish; I was not able to complete the limit bag of eight fish.

My next noteable success was on opening day, 24 March 1978, at Siblyback Lake. Feeling like a new man fully recovered from the bypass operation, I arrived at 0800 hours, dropped a batch of flies to Lawrence Emmett the warden and had a word about fish stocking – then went off to try my luck. As the wind was blowing down from the dam towards the little marsh, being left-handed, I decided to fish down from the feeder stream on the opposite bank to the small marsh.

Using a slow sinking shooting head casting thirty yards plus and giving it twenty to thirty seconds to sink, I stripped the Michael's Streamer back fast. On the third cast I had a good solid take and eventually netted a good condition brown trout of 1³/₄ lbs. Gradually fished my way up to the point which is about halfway between the two marshes. It was here I had a take and played out a nice rainbow of 4 lb 3 oz, which put a bit of a tangle in my shooting backing line which took a bit of time to sort out.

Fishing on, and after leaving one streamer in the bottom of the lake, I tied on another Michael's Streamer. On the very next cast while I was waiting for the line to sink, a fish seized the streamer on the drop. On its first run the fish came straight towards me and although I was hand stripping line as fast as I could I was having great difficulty keeping in touch. The fish came right in close, spotted me, turned and made a sizzling run towards the middle of the lake, taking out about thirty yards of line. The fish looked to be in the five pound range, and for a while it stayed thirty yards out cruising up and down, at times making short boring runs and then coming to the surface with a splash. It then made another run towards me so fast that I was not able to stay in touch. Turning again it sizzled out, pulling line through my fingers. To my horror I saw my backing line had tangled up and a great clump was going through the rod rings. Fortunately I turned the fish before this tangle went out through the top ring. Gently I recovered line working this tangle back through the rings. Gradually getting the fish under control, I started putting pressure on it; after about five minutes of lively aerobatics and short boring runs, I brought the fish to the surface on its side and slid the landing net safely under it – a beautiful fish of 4 lb 7 oz. It was a very good start to the season.

The next series of streamer flies have taken fish all over the world, including both Atlantic and Pacific salmon and they are very popular with trout and sea trout anglers. The flies are American in origin; I do not know who the inventors are.

Black Ghost Streamer – *USA* – (*Plate 14*)
Tail   Golden pheasant crest
Body   Black wool silver rib
Hackle   Golden pheasant crest or yellow hackle
Wing   Four white hackles
Cheeks   Jungle cock

Grey Ghost Streamer – *USA* – (*Plate 14*)
Body   Orange wool
Hackle   Strands of bronze peacock herl, then white bucktail, finally dyed yellow hackle
   fibres
Wing   Four blue dun hackles
Cheeks   Lady Amherst tippet

Brown Ghost Streamer – *USA* – (*Plate 14*)
Tag   Silver tinsel
Body   Brown wool silver rib
Hackle   Strands of bronze peacock herl, then white bucktail, finally golden crest
Wing   Four red game hackles with golden pheasant topping over
Shoulder   Teal flank dyed brown
Cheeks   Jungle cock

Royal Coachman Streamer (*Plate 14*)
Tail   Golden pheasant tippets
Body   In three parts; peacock herl/red floss/peacock herl
Wing   Four white cock hackles
Hackle   Red game cock

Parmachene Belle Streamer – *USA* – (*Plate 14*)
Tail   Married red and yellow – goose or duck feather slips
Body   Yellow wool ribbed gold oval
Wing   Two white cock hackles with two dyed red hackles outside, two-thirds the size
Hackle   Dyed red mixed with white cock hackle

Chief Needabeh Streamer – *USA* – (*Plate 14*)
Tag   Silver tinsel
Body   Scarlet floss ribbed oval tinsel silver
Wing   Two dyed yellow with two dyed orange hackles outside
Hackle   Dyed yellow and scarlet cock
Cheeks   Jungle cock

Orange Badger Streamer – *USA* – (*Plate 14*)
Tail   Dyed red cock fibres
Body   Gold tinsel ribbed gold oval
Wing   Two badger hackles dyed hot orange
Hackle   Dyed red cock

Marabou-winged Lures

The next series of lures are winged with marabou; this is soft fluffy feather fibre which has a good action in water and imparts life to the lure.

Crowdy Marsh Marabou Lure (*Plate 15*)
Tail Orange marabou
Body Two parts: 1st oval silver, 2nd orange marabou
Wings Black marabou
Hackle Dyed yellow cock

Black and Orange Marabou Lure (*Plate 15*)
Tail Orange marabou
Body Size 17 oval silver tinsel
Wings Black marabou
Hackle Orange marabou

Black Marabou Lure (*Plate 15*)
Body Black ostrich herl, ribbed silver oval
Wings Black marabou
Hackle Black cock

Black Marabou and Peacock Lure (*Plate 15*)
Tail Dyed red cock fibres
Body Peacock herl
Wings Black marabou
Hackle Black cock

White Marabou Lure
Tail Dyed orange cock fibres
Body D.F.M. white wool, ribbed silver oval
Wing White marabou
Hackle Teal flank

Appetiser – *R. Church*
Tail Green, orange, red, dyed cock hackle fibres, and teal flank fibres
Body White chenille ribbed silver oval
Wing White marabou with grey squirrel over
Hackle Green, orange, red, dyed cock fibres and teal flank fibres

The Appetiser is very useful when there are fry about in the reservoir. However it will take trout throughout the season. A great favourite with many anglers and can be used with confidence on all types of water.

Hair Wing Lures

For the hair wing and streamer lures (*see page 80*) any longshank size hook can be used, but I prefer to dress them in size 6 or 8.

Yellowbelly Lure (*Plate 15*)
Tail Dyed bright red cock fibres
Tag D.F.M scarlet wool
Body Yellow chenille
Wing Brown calf tail
Hackle Dyed red cock

Grey Squirrel Lure (*Plate 15*)
Tail Dyed yellow cock fibres
Tag D.F.M. green wool
Body Grey chenille
Wing Grey squirrel tail
Hackle Badger

D.F.M. Black cock fibres *(Plate 15)*
Tail Black cock fibres
Body First third D.F.M. scarlet wool then black chenille
Wing Black squirrel tail flanked with dyed orange goose
Hackle Black cock

The D.F.M. black lure is very effective at the beginning of the season and usually can be relied on to take fish throughout. The method of fishing is the same as other lures; special attention needs to be given when fishing it on the sinking line for on-the-drop takes.

D.F.M. Black and Green Lure *(Plate 15)*
Tail Teal flank
Body First third D.F.M. green wool then brown chenille
Wing Black squirrel tail
Hackle Black cock

Black Chenille Lure *(Plate 15)*
Tail Black cock hackle fibres
Body Black chenille
Wing Black squirrel tail
Hackle Black cock

Sweeny Todd – *Richard Walker* – *(Plate 15)*
Tying silk Black
Body Black floss or wool, ribbed silver oval tinsel
Throat Magenta fluorescent wool
Wing Natural black squirrel tail
Hackle Dyed bright red cock

Killer Wing Style

Trevadlock Killer *(Plate 13)*
Tail Grey squirrel tail hair
Body D.F.M. yellow wool
Wing Four teal flank feathers, dressed killer style
Hook Size 6, longshank

D.F.M. Scarlet Killer *(Plate 13)*
Tail Grey squirrel tail hair dyed green highlander
Body D.F.M. scarlet wool
Wing Four brown mallard shoulder feathers, dressed killer style
Hook Size 6, longshank

D.F.M. Partridge Killer *(Plate 15)*
Tail Black squirrel tail hair
Body D.F.M. yellow wool
Wing Four brown partridge hackles, dressed killer style
Hook Size 8 or 6, longshank

Elver Eel *(Plate 15)*
Tail Two jungle cock saddle hackles back to back
Body Wool, any colour
Wing Two jungle cock saddle, dressed killer style

The elver pattern can be dressed with any colour body or wing. The grey-white list of the jungle cock saddle hackle can be coloured with felt tip pen thus creating any colour combination. I usually dye the saddle cape blue and dress a blue elver with a silver tinsel body – useful for fresh run sea trout and salmon.

The Leadhead Lure

To tie the leadhead or metal bead fly pinch the leadshot or bead on the hookshank behind the hookeye and coat it with whatever colour varnish is required. After the varnish is dry, dress the body in the normal manner. Tie in the marabou fibres just behind the metal head so that it encircles the hookshank like a collar, now add a few strands of Flashabou to the marabou. Tie a neat head right up close to the metal bead and then varnish the head and bead together.

Most of the takes will come while the lure sinks after being cast out. The metal head will cause the lure to dive head first and the fluttering of the marabou fibres with the erratic sinking action makes it attractive and the fish will really hit the lure. These lures are tricky to cast on light tackle as the weight of the lure makes smooth casting impossible so you have to slow down the line speed.

The hooksizes are the tyer's own choice, as are the size of the metal head; all sizes are effective.

Black Leadhead
Body   Black wool
Wing   Marabou black fibres with silver Flashabou
Head   Leadshot or metal bead

Yellow Leadhead
Body   Yellow wool
Wing   Yellow marabou fibres with Flashabou
Head   Leadshot or metal bead

Orange Leadhead
Body   Orange wool
Wing   Orange marabou fibres with red Flashabou
Head   Leadshot or metal bead

Tadpole Lure
Tail   Marabou fibres dyed black
Hackle   Black cock
Head   Chenille (muddler style)
Hook   Size 8, longshank

Tadpoles are simple to imitate. First wind the black silk half way down the hookshank tying in the marabou tail as you do so. Wind the silk back up the hookshank thus forming a pencil-slim body. Tie a long fibre black cock hackle in near the hookeye. Wind the hackle at least six times then secure, pulling the fibres back towards the tail thus veiling the body completely, and overtie, making sure there is enough room for the muddler type head. Tie in the chenille and complete the lure.

Floating Lures

It is nearly always assumed that streamer and hair wing lures are fished under the surface. This is not the case with specialist patterns that are fished so as to cause a disturbance on the surface, like a wounded or crippled minnow, which will bring up the hungry predator to slash at the lure. For floating lures I use buoyant material such as deer hair, cork, balsa wood or polyurethane foam.

A method of fishing I find successful when the lake trout are coming into the shallows chasing fry is to allow the lure to float with natural water movement and then give it a twitch or two.

Other creatures can be imitated and fished on the surface, such as frogs, grasshoppers, stoneflies and crickets and I have devised the following to imitate them. How you fish these floating lures is important and careful observation of crippled or stunned minnows will help you to impart realistic movement. I like to give the line a short jerk thus causing the lure to go under the water and pop up again; this can be very effective at times, bringing fish from quite a distance. Very often the first thing you become aware of is a bow wave heading for your lure at speed; it is quite a problem to choose between moving the lure or leaving it floating still, and exciting fishing can be had from such tactics. The trying of my specialist floating patterns are very time consuming and they cannot be dressed on a commercial basis – but for the amateur time may be not so important, so try a few of the dressings.

Minnow Surface Lure
Tail   Grey white bucktail clipped fishtail shape
Body   Cork slips whipped on hookshank covered with silver white, raffia wound to a fish-like shape, ribbed wide silver tinsel and varnished
Head   Deer hair – first a pinch of dyed red hair followed by natural colour deer hair
Hook   Size 8 or 6, longshank

To tie the floating minnow, wind the silk down the hookshank leaving the first part clear for spinning the deer hair. Tie in the bucktail for the length of the silk-covered hookshank, clip the loose end of the bucktail to a fishlike tail. Now tie in the cork slips each side of the hookshank; overtie the cork with plenty of turns with the silk to make the body really secure. Tie in raffia and silver tinsel, wind the raffia into a streamlined fish shape and rib with silver tinsel and then varnish liberally. When the varnish is dry, first spin in a pinch of dyed red deer hair to simulate the red of the gills, then complete the head with light coloured natural hair and clip the hair to match the taper of the body with a torpedo point to the head; leave some of the longer hair at the side just in front of the body to simulate fins.

Grasshopper Lure
Body   Yellow-green dyed deer hair, clipped to grasshopper body shape
Wing   Brown bucktail trimmed square with rear end of body
Hackle   Grizzle cock dyed green and clipped

Dress deer hair body in the normal manner and clip. For tying in the bucktail wing it is important that you build the silk bed foundation up level with the deer hair body so that the bucktail will lie level. If you leave any sort of step down from the deer hair body, as you pull your first turn of silk tight while tying in the bucktail, it will flare up and you will have the individual hairs pointing in all directions. Make sure the foundation is as high or slightly higher than the body, tie in the bucktail with two or three loose turns of silk and gently pull tight. Clip the grizzle hackle to within 1.25 cm (¹/₂ in) of the hookshank. The hooksize can be longshank size six to ten – anything smaller would be the same as a normal sedge fly. I consider the best size to be a light wire longshank size six.

Frog Surface Lure

Legs Bucktail twisted, secure at the end with fuse wire and the whipping varnished
Body Spun deer hair trimmed to frog shape and coloured with felt pen

Use a size two or four lightwire longshank hook. Wind on a few turns of silk at the hookbend. Lay your bucktail on the hookshank so that the turns of silk are about halfway up its length; now tie it in with a few turns of silk, double the bucktail hair back and twist the two ends together; secure the ends with fuse wire leaving enough hair to form the frog's feet. When the two rear legs are completed varnish the two whippings and the turns of silk on the hookshank. Now spin the deer hair body in the normal manner and clip to shape. Complete the front legs by the same method; colour body with felt pen.

Stone Hopper Lure

Tail Dyed red bucktail clipped square and short
Body Slips of cork, overtied with yellow silk
Wing Grey squirrel tail hair flanked by mottled turkey
Head Natural deer hair clipped

My Stone Hopper dressing is a useful general attractor pattern – very effective fished in a fast streamy run. It will bring trout up from quite a depth; even the lordly salmon will move itself for it.

Brown Wake Fly

Tail Dyed red bucktail clipped square
Wing Grey squirrel tail hair flanked by brown turkey rump
Head Dyed brown deer hair partly clipped

White Wake Fly

Tail Dyed red bucktail clipped square
Wing White bucktail flanked by grey turkey
Head White deer hair partly clipped

Dress the wake flies on longshank size six hooks. Tie the bucktail hair tail so that it encircles the hookshank making it possible to overtie with tight turns of silk, thus making a lightweight body. Clip the tail square across about 2.5 cm (1 in) long. Leave the deer hair head quite bushy, trimming it so that it tapers down towards the hookeye.

Fish the wake fly with long slow pulls so that they leave a wake across the surface of the water. When the fish chase them you will see a big bow wave coming up behind the lure.

9

The Salmon Fly

Salmon flies can be classified into three groupings: the traditional fully dressed salmon fly; the more recent hairwing fly which has become very popular; and the tube fly and Waddington Shank flies.

The fully dressed salmon fly, properly tied, is a work of great beauty and an art form in its own right. To be able to dress the traditional patterns correctly requires a good knowledge of the materials used and the ability to handle them skilfully.

Because of the nature of their wing construction the traditional flies can be divided into several groups:

1 *Plain feather strip wings*   These are formed by taking feather slips from right and left hand quills. With soft feathers like brown mallard shoulders or teal flanks the wings can be formed by taking two slips from the same side of the feather, placing them on top of each other and folding, thus forming the wing.

2 *Herl wings*   The herls from the sword (green herl) and eye (bronze herl) of a peacock tail feather makes the wings for some very useful salmon patterns.

3 *Golden topping wings*   These wings are formed entirely of a bunch of toppings which come from the back of a golden pheasant cock's head.

4 *Mixed feather fibre wings*   The mixed wings are created by marrying together fibres of several different feathers, or goose shoulders dyed various bright colours. A right and left hand side of the wing are formed and tied into the fly like a normal wing.

5 *Built wings*   This is a wing that is tied with mixed wings over strip or whole feather wings, plus married strips of brown mallard, teal flank and summer duck or grey mallard on the sides, finally macaw horns, jungle cock eyes, blue chatterer cheeks and golden pheasant toppings over the lot; quite an undertaking requiring considerable skill to produce the perfectly dressed example of the flytyer's craft.

There are not many examples of the traditional fully dressed fly in all its glory being used for fishing; they usually end up by being framed and hung on the wall. The present day mode is for lightly dressed slim flies that sink well and do not skate across the surface as a more heavily dressed fly would do. To achieve slim fish-catching flies that do not skate if properly used, but still follow the traditional style (allowing for the fact that many of the traditional tying materials are no longer readily available) I have devised the following variations of the traditional fully dressed patterns. To dress my variations, which are really just a pale reflection of the splendour of the originals, however, requires the same basic knowledge and tying techniques.

Jock Scott – *Traditional*
Tag   Silver tinsel yellow floss

Tail   Golden pheasant topping, indian crow
Butt   Black ostrich herl
Body   In two equal parts: No 1 yellow floss ribbed silver oval tinsel, butted toucan and
   black ostrich herl; No 2 black floss, ribbed silver oval tinsel with black hackle over
Throat   Guinea fowl hackle
Wings   Two strips of dark mottled turkey, golden pheasant tail, yellow-red-blue swan,
   bustard, peacock wing, married narrow strips of brown and grey mallard, two strands of
   peacock sword feather, toppings.
Sides   Jungle cock
Cheeks   Blue chatterer
Horns   Blue Macaw
Head   Black silk

Jock Scott – *Variation*
Tag   Silver tinsel yellow floss
Tail   Topping, indian crow
Butt   Black wool dubbed on silk
Body   No 1 Yellow Floss ribbed silver oval; No 2 black seal's fur ribbed silver tinsel, black
   hackle over
Throat   Guinea fowl
Wings   Two strips brown turkey, strands peacock sword, yellow-red-blue goose, married
   brown mallard and teal, topping over
Sides   Jungle cock

The difference between the two dressings shows how much material can be
dispensed with. If the tyer so chooses, the dressing can be reduced even further;
however there would be no point in calling it a Jock Scott, just a special.

Now to explain some of the techniques used to dress these flies: first of all we will
start with preparing the married wings.
   To select the fibres for marrying, hold the quill so that you are looking at the
weather side of the feather, taking the fibres from the same side of the quills held in
such a fashion; they now can be married together to form one side of the married
wing, which we can assume will be the left hand side. Picking the quills for right
hand side you will need to be looking at the weather side of the feather with the
fibres on the right hand side of the quill. Select the fibres and marry together to
form the right hand side of the mixed wing. The technique for marrying fibres
together is quite straightforward: take up each fibre separately and lay on top of
each other, keeping the tips together; hold the tips together and, grasping the
butts, pull taut together, which will cause the little hooks to interlock and marry
the fibres together; continue adding fibres to the wing until completed. All it will
then require is a little stroking at the ends to make a neat job; it is the same as
anything else, only practise will make perfection possible. You cannot mix your
fibres, right hand fibres will not marry with left hand fibres; if you do make a
mistake and try it you will notice they just fall apart. Some fibres will marry quite
easily, e.g., goose shoulders, turkey rumps, Florican bustard and speckled bustard. The wild fowl and game birds are more difficult, particularly brown mallard
shoulders and teal if being married to turkey or goose, although they marry quite
easily together.

Now to tie a mixed wing variant.

Kate
Tag   Silver tinsel, yellow floss
Tail   Topping
Butt   Black wool, dubbed
Body   Crimson seal's fur, ribbed silver tinsel with crimson hackle over
Throat   Yellow cock
Wing   Married bustard, yellow-crimson-light blue goose, brown mallard, topping
Sides   Jungle cock

Wind the silk from eye to hook bend, laying down a good foundation. Tie in silver tinsel and form tag and give it a coat of varnish; tie in yellow floss and wind to complete the tag. Select a couple of small toppings with a good curve and tie in one on top of the other thus making a bold-looking tail. Dub black wool on the tying silk to form the butt so as to hide where the topping has been tied in. Tie in tinsel rib and then dub crimson seal's fur on the silk and form the body. Select crimson hackle and prepare tip for tying in, spreading the hackle fibres to the right angle of the stalk. Lay the hackle tip on top of the hook near one butt end, wind the tinsel rib, thus trapping the hackle tip on top of the body. After ribbing the body, tie in the tinsel but do not cut off. Now double the hackle by stroking fibres together with finger and thumb – a little saliva may help to accomplish the doubling by making the fibres stick together. Wind the hackle close to the tinsel rib, stroking the fibres backward, making sure the hackle stays double. When complete tie in and trim off surplus hackle and tinsel together. The reason for not cutting the tinsel off earlier is that should the hackle break or slip from under the tinsel rib it would be easy to start again.

Tie in the dyed yellow throat hackle and wind, tie it down and stroke back fibres and secure, thus making a level foundation for winging. Place the two sides of the married wings together making sure the tips line up and they are of equal width. If all is well now tie them in.

Prepare the jungle cock eyes and tie in; trim off surplus wing fibres and jungle cock eyes stalks; prepare the topping for tying in by removing the fibres from the base and making a little step in the stalk with hackle pliers. Putting the step in the stalk helps to tie the topping in properly over the wing; it ensures it is straight and stops any twisting and moving about during the tying in operation.

There are various methods for imparting a curve to golden pheasant crests that have become twisted or crushed in storage. One method is to moisten them and stick them into a smooth tumbler, making sure they lie in the circumference of the glass, not sloping up or down. When they are dry they will fall to the bottom of the glass, retaining the curve imparted by the shape of the glass. The only disadvantage of this method is that different size glasses have to be used for the different size toppings required. My method is more direct; I borrow my wife's hair curling tongs. Moistening the toppings, I will curl them to whatever shape or size required, but be careful not to allow the electric tongs to become too hot as toppings are quite delicate and will not take too much heat of that kind. I usually shape a dozen or so at a time.

Another useful fly-tying tip, when tying in jungle cock eyes and blue chatterer cheeks, is to moisten the fibres of the blue chatterer feather and stick it on top of the jungle cock feather. This makes it possible to tie both feathers in together, thus reducing the numbers of turns of silk needed, which in turn reduces the bulk of the head of the fly.

Mixed Wing Variants

Childers (*Plate 16*)
Tag   Silver tinsel, blue floss
Tail   Topping
Body   Light yellow first part, then red seal's fur, ribbed silver oval
Hackle   Dyed yellow cock
Throat   Red hackle and strands of widgeon
Wings   Red-blue goose, brown turkey, brown mallard, topping
Cheeks   Blue chatterer

Dixon (*Plate 16*)
Tag   Gold tinsel, yellow floss
Tail   Topping
Body   Orange seal's fur, ribbed gold tinsel
Hackle   Claret
Throat   Guinea fowl
Wing   Red-blue-yellow goose, golden pheasant tail
Sides   Brown mallard and summer duck, topping over

Silver Doctor (*Plate 16*)
Tag   Silver tinsel, yellow floss
Tail   Topping
Butt   Scarlet wool
Body   Silver tinsel, ribbed silver oval
Throat   Blue hackle and guinea fowl
Wings   Yellow-red-blue goose, golden pheasant
Sides   Married brown mallard and summer duck with topping over
Head   Red silk, clear varnished

Silver Grey (*Plate 16*)
Tag   Silver tinsel, yellow floss
Tail   Topping
Butt   Black wool
Body   Silver tinsel, ribbed silver oval
Hackle   Badger cock
Throat   Widgeon flank
Wings   White-yellow-blue-green goose, brown mallard
Sides   Married grey mallard and summer duck with topping over

Torrish (*Plate 16*)
Tag   Silver tinsel, yellow floss
Tail   Topping, ibis
Butt   Black wool
Body   Silver tinsel in two parts, first part butted with dyed red hackle that has been wound and swept back so as to veil the silver, second part silver tinsel, ribbed silver oval
Throat   Hot orange hackle
Wings   Red-blue-orange goose, peacock wing, brown mallard with topping over

White Doctor (*Plate 16*)
Tag   Silver tinsel, yellow floss
Tail   Topping
Butt   Scarlet wool
Body   D.F.M. white wool, ribbed silver oval
Hackle   Dyed pale blue
Throat   Dyed blue guinea fowl
Wings   Yellow-red-blue-green goose, brown mallard

Sides Guinea fowl
Cheeks Blue chatterer
Head Red silk, clear varnished

Strip Wing Variants

Akroyd (*Plate 16*)
Tag Gold tinsel
Tail Topping
Body First part yellow seal's fur followed by black seal's fur, ribbed gold oval
Throat Black hackle
Wings Cinnamon turkey tail
Sides Jungle cock

Badger (*Plate 16*)
Tag Silver tinsel
Tail Topping
Body Crimson seal's fur, ribbed silver tinsel
Throat Silver badger hackle
Wings Light mottled turkey tail

Chalmers (*Plate 16*)
Tag Silver tinsel
Tail Topping
Body D.F.M. magenta wool, ribbed silver tinsel
Throat Magenta hackle
Wings Dark mottled turkey tail
Sides Jungle cock

Dunkeld (*Plate 16*)
Tag Gold tinsel
Tail Topping
Body Gold tinsel, ribbed gold oval
Hackle Hot orange
Throat Blue jay
Wings Brown mallard
Cheeks Blue chatterer

Fiery Brown
Tag Gold tinsel
Tail Topping
Body Fiery brown seal's fur, ribbed gold oval
Hackle Fiery brown
Throat Fiery brown
Wings Brown mallard

Thunder and Lightning (*Plate 16*)
Tag Gold tinsel, orange floss
Tail Topping
Body Black wool, ribbed gold oval
Hackle Hot orange
Throat Blue jay
Wings Brown mallard with topping over
Sides Jungle cock

Whole Feather Winged

Durham Ranger
Tag Silver tinsel, yellow floss

Tail Topping, indian crow
Butt Black wool
Body Two parts, first orange seal's fur then black seal's fur, ribbed silver oval
Hackle Hot orange
Throat Light blue hackle
Wing Four tippets overlapping two each side, enveloping two projecting jungle cock eyes, topping over
Cheeks Blue chatterer

Avon Eagle (*Plate 16*)
Tag Silver tinsel
Tail Topping
Body Lemon-orange-scarlet-fiery brown seal's fur in equal parts
Rib Broad silver tinsel
Throat Yellow turkey marabou and teal
Wing Golden pheasant red rump feathers, two or three topping over
Side Jungle cock

Dennison (*Plate 16*)
Tag Silver tinsel
Tail Topping
Body Two parts, first silver tinsel, then pale blue floss ribbed silver oval
Hackle Light blue cock
Throat Blue jay
Wing Two tippets enveloping two jungle cock hackles, veiled with two golden pheasant yellow rump feathers with topping over
Sides Teal
Head Black ostrich herl

Orange Parson (*Plate 16*)
Tag Silver tinsel, lilac floss
Tail Topping
Body Orange seal's fur, ribbed silver oval
Hackle Lemon
Throat Orange hackle
Wings Tippets back to back veiled with hot orange hackles, topping over
Sides Summer duck
Cheeks Blue chatterer

Silver Fairy
Tail Amherst pheasant toppings
Body Embossed silver tinsel, ribbed silver oval
Hackle White
Throat White hackle
Wings Amherst pheasant tippets
Sides Jungle cock

Canary (*Plate 16*)
Tag Gold tinsel
Tail Topping, indian crow
Body Silver tinsel, ribbed silver oval
Hackle Yellow
Throat Orange hackle
Wings Six golden pheasant toppings

Variegated Sun Fly
Tag　Silver tinsel, blue floss
Tail　Topping, orange hackle strands
Body　Black, orange and yellow wool (wound together)
Throat　Black hackle

To dress golden pheasant crest wings it is important that all the topping stems are flattened and a step made at the point where the initial silk turn is made. Also the stems must be tied on top of each other; it is better if they are all tied in together but if this should be difficult they can be tied in singly. Very often the topping will tie in easily if they are prepared for tying in by selecting the smallest for the base and the rest gradually increasing in size until the top and final crest is in position, then moistened.

Herl Wing Flies

Beauly Snow Fly
Body　Pale blue seal's fur
Rib　Silver tinsel and gold twist
Hackle　Black cock from third turn of twist
Wings　Bronze herl from peacock eye
Head　Hot orange hackle dressed as a collar

Green Peacock
Tag　Silver tinsel, yellow floss
Tail　Topping
Body　Blue floss ribbed silver oval
Throat　Pale blue hackle
Wings　Peacock sword feather

Lovat
Tag　Silver tinsel
Tail　Golden pheasant red breast hackle
Body　Two turns yellow wool followed by blue wool
Hackle　Black cock
Wings　Bronze peacock herl
Head　Yellow hackle dressed as collar

Low Water Patterns

All patterns can be used for low water conditions providing that they are lightly dressed. There is a mode of tying for these conditions when they occur, the chief characteristics of which are light wire hooks, short light bodies which dress only half of the hookshank, plus narrow short wings. The following dressings are normally the most popular and are fished on floating lines with leaders of 3.5 kg (8 lb) breaking strain.

Claret Alder (*Plate 18*)
Tag　Silver tinsel, orange floss
Tail　Claret wool
Body　Peacock herl, ribbed gold oval
Throat　Dark claret hackle
Wings　Brown mallard

Blue Charm (*Plate 18*)
Tag   Silver tinsel
Tail   Topping
Body   Black floss, ribbed silver oval
Throat   Blue hackle
Wings   Brown mallard with narrow strips of teal on the sides, topping over all

Blue Peacock
Tail   Red ibis
Body   Silver tinsel, ribbed silver oval
Hackle   Blue peacock, dressed as collar and swept back so as to veil the silver body

Silver Blue
Tag   Silver tinsel
Tail   Topping
Body   Silver tinsel, ribbed silver oval
Throat   Blue hackle
Wings   Teal

Logie (*Plate 18*)
Tag   Silver tinsel
Tail   Topping
Body   First part primrose floss, remainder red floss, ribbed silver oval
Throat   Pale blue hackle
Wing   Yellow goose flanked strips of brown mallard

Skirmisher (*Plate 18*)
Tag   Silver tinsel
Tail   Ibis
Body   Orange floss, ribbed silver oval
Throat   Furnace hackle
Wing   Golden pheasant flanked ibis and teal

Sir Charles (*Plate 18*)
Tag   Silver tinsel
Tail   Topping
Body   Golden yellow floss, ribbed silver oval
Throat   Pale blue cock
Wing   Peacock sword flanked by teal

Jockie (*Plate 18*)
Tag   Silver tinsel
Tail   Topping
Body   First third golden yellow floss, remainder dark claret floss, ribbed silver oval
Throat   Furnace hackle
Wing   Brown mallard

Badger
Tag   Silver tinsel
Tail   Topping
Body   Crimson floss, ribbed silver oval
Throat   Badger hackle
Wing   Light mottle turkey

Black Fairy
Tag   Gold tinsel, yellow floss
Tail   Topping
Body   Black floss, ribbed gold oval

Throat   Black hackle
Wing   Brown mallard

Hair Wing Flies

Salmon hair wing flies have become popular because they are effective and easy to tie when compared to the dressing of the traditional feather patterns; the hair wing can be tied to a passable standard by any tyer who has the basic knowledge and tying skill. Over the last few years this has led to a proliferation of patterns, many of which have been short lived and have not stood the test of time.

Therefore I list the more effective tyings, with some variations, with dressings based on the traditional feathered patterns. On some of my patterns I like to flank the hair wing with a narrow strip of dyed goose shoulder. I also use feather slips from white duck quills tied in short so as to simulate jungle cock eyes. For the bodies, in place of the double hackle which is dressed palmer fashion, I complete the first half of body and rib, then tie in a hackle – wind it and sweep the fibres back so that it veils the body already dressed. Completing the body, I tie in the throat hackle and wind, sweeping back the fibres so as to veil the front half of the fly body. This is where the long-fibred hackles of game and other birds come into good use; they envelope the fly bodies and impart 'life' to the fly so that the fish cannot resist them. For the wing I use calf tail hair, except in the larger sizes when it becomes necessary to use bucktail. Added flash can be incorporated by mixing some strands of Flashabou into the hair of the wings.

When finishing off the hair wing, make sure you work plenty of varnish into the cut end of the wing before completing the head. The head will require a couple of coats of varnish followed by a couple of days to harden off. There is nothing more annoying than to have a fly start to break up after only a few casts.

Salmon will take the fly in various ways: on some occasions they take the fly so savagely that it gets chewed up quite badly; on other occasions they will just nip at the fly dressing without actually taking the hook into their mouths. It is very important not to dress the wing longer than the hookshank; although it will not stop the fish nipping the fly, the chance of hooking the fish is better than with a fly dressed with a long wing.

Black Dose
Tag   Orange floss
Tail   Topping
Body   First royal blue seal's fur, then black seal's fur, ribbed silver oval
Throat   Light claret hackle
Wing   Red-green-brown calf tail

Black Maria
Tag   Oval tinsel
Tail   Topping
Body   First half yellow floss, then black floss, ribbed silver oval
Throat   Black heron or substitute
Wing   Black calftail

Cosseboom (*Plate 17*)
Tag   Silver tinsel
Tail   Short olive floss

Body   Olive green floss, ribbed silver tinsel
Wing   Grey squirrel tail
Collar   Yellow hackle dressed as collar
Head   Red

Camel's Tail (*Plate 17*)
Tag   Red floss
Body   Gold tinsel, ribbed gold oval
Throat   Pheasant green rump
Wing   Yellow-light brown calf tail

Gilroy
Body   Black floss, ribbed silver oval
Wing   Black squirrel tail hair tied all round hookshank
Collar   Pale blue cock hackle

Goldie (*Plate 17*)
Tag   Gold tinsel, yellow floss
Tail   Hot orange bucktail
Butt   Black ostrich herl
Body   Rear half gold tinsel, butted yellow cock hackle, front half gold tinsel, ribbed gold
   oval
Throat   Yellow cock with red squirrel tail in front
Wing   Orange bucktail

Green Highlander
Tag   Silver tinsel
Tail   Topping
Body   Yellow floss then green highlander seal's fur, ribbed oval silver
Hackle   Green cock, palmer style
Throat   Yellow hackle
Wing   Orange-green calf tail

Hairy Mary
Tag   Gold tinsel
Tail   Topping
Body   Black wool, ribbed gold oval
Throat   Blue hackle
Wing   Brown calf tail

Hot Orange
Tag   Gold tinsel, yellow floss
Body   Black floss, ribbed gold oval
Throat   Hot orange hackle
Wing   Black squirrel tail

Logie (*Plate 17*)
Tag   Silver tinsel
Tail   Topping
Body   Rear primrose floss then red floss, ribbed silver tinsel
Throat   Blue hackle
Wing   Yellow-brown calftail

Munro Killer
Tag   Gold tinsel
Tail   Orange hackle tips
Body   Orange then black floss, ribbed gold tinsel

Hackle   Orange cock, palmer style
Throat   Guinea fowl dyed blue
Wing   Grey squirrel tail dyed yellow

Tartan
Tag   Gold tinsel
Tail   Golden pheasant yellow rump feather
Body   Orange and red seal's fur in equal parts, ribbed gold oval
Hackle   Blue, palmer style
Throat   Grizzle and red hackles
Wing   Grey squirrel

Willie Gunn (*Plate 17*)
Body   Black floss, ribbed gold oval
Wing   Orange-yellow-black bucktail mixed, tied in all around hookshank

Yellow Torrish (*Plate 17*)
Tag   Silver tinsel, yellow floss
Tail   Topping
Butt   Black ostrich
Body   Silver tinsel, ribbed silver oval
Throat   Yellow hackle
Wing   Yellow-brown calf tail

West Country Patterns

The following three dressings are patterns I have devised for the rivers of Cornwall and Devon. I have included the plastic tinsel in the wing which gives the flies added flash and I believe it is this that makes them so effective.

Trudie (*Plate 17*)
Tail   Yellow D.F.M. wool
Body   Copper tinsel, ribbed copper wire
Hackle   Golden pheasant yellow rump
Wing   Light brown calf tail mixed with copper Flashabou
Sides   Jungle cock or substitute

Wendy (*Plate 17*)
Tail   Green D.F.M. wool
Body   Copper tinsel, ribbed silverwire
Hackle   Golden pheasant red breast
Wing   Brown calf tail mixed with gold Flashabou
Sides   Jungle cock or substitute

Gwendoline (*Plate 17*)
Tail   Red wool
Body   Two parts, first red wool followed by light blue wool
Hackle   Orange cock
Wing   Red-silver-blue Flashabou mixed natural red tail hair

The following series of salmon flies were given to me by Michael Summers of Devon Flies. These hair wing dressings are West Country patterns and will take fish on all the rivers in the region; also when dressed on small hooks they are quite effective for sea trout.

Black Tamish (*Plate 17*)
Tag   Embossed silver tinsel

Tail   Red wool or floss
Body   Black wool or floss
Rib   Embossed silver tinsel
Wing   Grey squirrel tail
Hackle   Black cock wound as collar, swept back and overtied thus veiling the squirrel hair
   wing
Cheeks   Jungle cock
Head   Red silk

Orange Tamish (*Plate 17*)
Tag   Flat gold tinsel
Tail   Red silk or wool
Body   Orange wool or floss
Rib   Flat gold tinsel
Wing   Grey and black squirrel hair mixed
Hackle   Black cock wound as collar veiling the wing
Cheeks   Jungle cock
Head   Black

Red/Orange Tamish (*Plate 17*)
Tag   Flat gold tinsel
Tail   Red floss or wool
Body   Orange floss or wool
Rib   Flat gold tinsel
Wing   Black-orange-red goat hair mixed
Hackle   Black cock wound as collar veiling the wing
Cheeks   Jungle cock
Head   Red silk

Jungle Stoat (*Plate 17*)
Tag   Silver oval
Tail   Topping
Body   Black floss or wool
Rib   Silver tinsel
Wing   Black squirrel
Hackle   Dyed blue guinea fowl
Cheeks   Jungle cock
Head   Black

Silver Dart (*Plate 17*)
Tag   Fine oval silver tinsel
Tip   Orange floss
Tail   Topping
Butt   Bronze peacock herl
Body   Two parts, rear two-thirds flat silver tinsel, then black floss
Rib   Silver oval
Wing   Grey squirrel
Hackle   Grizzle tied as collar
Cheeks   Jungle cock
Head   Red silk

Black Dart (*Plate 17*)
Tail   Black squirrel
Body   Black floss or wool
Rib   Embossed silver tinsel

Wing   Black squirrel extending to end of tail (both tail and wing very sparse)
Hackle   Black cock

The traditional and hair wing flies are dressed on loop-eyed single or double hooks, ranging from size twelve up to 5/0. Normally it is not necessary to dress them on any size larger than 1/0; if larger flies are required the tube or Waddington type fly will probably suit better.

On the single hooks I form my tinsel tags using Lurex tinsel which I varnish to improve durability. For the double hooks I use oval tinsel which is better suited to the shape of the double at the tail end. To tie a tinsel tag on a double hook, first whip on the silk foundation. Tie in the oval tinsel; instead of winding the tinsel in touching turns working up the body as you would do dressing a normal fly, wind the tinsel in touching turns towards the hook-bend; when the tag is wide enough, pass the loose end of the oval tinsel between the vee of the double hook, doubling it back over the tag and tying it with a couple turns of silk; pull it tight and secure with more turns of silk. Varnishing the oval tinsel will improve durability and prevent the tag from tarnishing.

It is very easy to overdress the wing of a hair wing fly, particularly if there are several different colours to be tied in. If for example I was dressing a hair wing with bucktail requiring four colours for the wing, I would not use more than eight hairs per colour, probably less, depending a little on the pattern. However eight hairs in four colours would give a wing of thirty-two strands of hair which makes quite a good wing. The density of individual animal's tail hair varies quite considerably and my hair wing is only intended as a general guide; adjust the wing density to your fancy.

When dressing a multi-colour hair wing I like to tie the colours in separately – it gives the wing more 'life' in the whole effect than a wing where the hair has been dressed all in one operation. I dress my wing by adding the colours on top of each other. When I add the next bunch of hair on top of the turns of silk below – I make sure the first two turns of silk are directly on top of the turns of silk below, the third turn I take behind them, thus pulling the bunch of hair directly down on the different colour hair below it, using the loop over the top technique – the same method as for tying a feathered wing (see page 19). Continue this until the full colour of the wing is completed, trim off surplus hair by cutting it at an angle so it is possible to finish off with a neat tapered head. This technique of dressing multi-colour wings can bulk up the head if too many turns of silk are used, but with a little practise it is surprising how well the hair will stay in position with only one or two turns of silk during the tying operation. The pattern that requires the hair wing to encircle the body can be dressed by two methods: firstly this can be achieved by tying on little bunches of hair around the hookshank; the other technique is to take a large bunch of hair, secure loosely on the hookshank with a couple of turns of silk and then spread the hair with finger and thumb. With a little practise you will find that this is probably the best technique.

10

Tubes, Waddingtons and Special Flies

The tube fly is the name given to a pattern which is dressed on a length of fine tubing which is slid down a nylon cast until stopped by the eye of a treble hook. With the smaller tubes where the hookeye will not fix inside the tube, a small piece of bicycle valve rubber must be fixed over its end so that the treble hook can be held in line with the tube. There are tubes which are specially manufactured for fly-tying. These are made of plastic with moulded ends to prevent the dressing from slipping off, and have a cavity in the tail to take the eye of the treble hook so that it is always in perfect alignment.

No special tools are required to dress tube flies, just some salmon hooks with the loop-eyes removed in sizes 4, 2, 2/0, and 4/0. To tie a tube fly place one of the eyeless salmon hooks in the fly-tying vice. Now press the tube onto the eyeless hook very firmly but not so hard as to damage the tube. Wind the silk on down the tube and then tie in the rib and body floss. It is important the tube is firmly pressed on the hookshank during the tying operation. If it should come loose and spin around you will have to start again.

After completing the body ensure there is a good silk layer for the foundation of the wing. Animal hair just whipped on a nylon base will not stay in position for long. Cut off a small bunch of hair, then add in small batches, twisting the tube on the hookshank for each batch. Trim off surplus hair from each batch before tying in the next; this enables the tyer to follow each tying stage without his view being obscured by splayed out ends of surplus hair. Carry on doing this until the whole circumference of the tube is covered. Tidy up the waste ends and give the head a good coat of varnish, complete head and whip finish. Some patterns may require a hackle in front of the wing; tie it in and wind so that it forms a collar, sweep back and overtie to form a neat head to the dressing. To improve the appearance of the tube I dress the treble hooks with a brightly dyed cock hackle which is tied in close to the hookeye and partly swept back. I consider this improves the 'taking' qualities of the tube fly.

The tube fly patterns that follow can be dressed on any size tube; I will leave it to the tyer to decide taking into account the water he intends to fish and at what time of the year, a very important factor if he intends to make a successful trip.

Black Tube
Treble   Black cock hackle
Body   Black floss, ribbed silver tinsel
Wing   Black bucktail

Black and Silver
Treble   Dyed bright red cock hackle
Body   Silver tinsel, ribbed oval
Wing   Black bucktail

Black and Copper
Treble Dyed bright red cock hackle
Body Silver tinsel, ribbed gold oval
Wing Black bucktail

Black and Orange
Treble Hot orange cock hackle
Body D.F.M. orange wool, ribbed gold oval
Wing Black bucktail

Blue and Silver *(Plate 18)*
Treble Dyed red hackle
Body Silver tinsel, ribbed silver oval
Wing Blue and brown bucktail mixed

Blue, Red and Silver
Treble Dyed red hackle
Body Silver tinsel, ribbed oval
Wing Red and blue bucktail mixed

Brown and Red
Treble Golden pheasant red breast
Body Red floss, ribbed gold oval
Wing Brown bucktail

Brown and Yellow
Treble Golden pheasant yellow rump
Body Yellow wool, ribbed gold oval
Wing Brown bucktail

Brown and Green
Treble Golden pheasant yellow rump
Body D.F.M. green wool, ribbed silver oval
Wing Brown bucktail

Brown, Yellow and Gold
Treble Dyed yellow hackle
Body Gold tinsel, ribbed oval
Wing Brown and yellow bucktail mixed

Green, Yellow and Gold
Treble Dyed yellow hackle
Body Gold tinsel ribbed oval
Wing Green and yellow bucktail

Orange and Gold
Treble Hot orange hackle
Body Gold tinsel, ribbed oval
Wing Orange and brown mixed

Orange Tube *(Plate 18)*
Treble Hot orange hackle
Body D.F.M. orange wool, ribbed gold oval
Wing Hot orange bucktail

Orange, Red and Black
Treble Red hackle
Body Black wool, ribbed silver oval
Wing Red and orange bucktail mixed

Waddington Shank Flies

For these dressings it is important that the wings of the tubes and Waddington Shank bodies are dressed long enough to mask the points of the treble hooks when they are in place. To make the fishing of the tubes more interesting change the different hackle colour trebles around, it sometimes makes a difference.

Waddington Shanks can be purchased in all sizes ranging from 10 mm ($^1/_2$ in) right through the scale up to 55 mm ($2^1/_2$ in). One end of the shank has a loop eye which enables the turle knot to be used, the other end has a short loop which makes it possible to slip the treble hook on. A short length of rubber or plastic is required on the tail-end of the shank to hold the treble hook in line. It pays to bind the short leg of the loop (where the treble has been placed) with silk or wire before slipping the tubing down to hold the hook in line. If at any time the treble should be damaged the nylon and wire can be taken off which makes hook replacement very simple. The shanks can be weighted for early season when it is necessary to get the fly deep in high and cold water conditions. Tails of wool or hackles can be dressed on the treble hooks for the Waddington flies if the tyer thinks its necessary.

Black Doctor
Tag　Red floss
Body　Black floss, ribbed silver oval
Wing　Red bucktail with black bucktail over

Blue Charm
Tag　Yellow floss
Body　Black floss, ribbed silver tinsel
Wing　Grey squirrel

Ruby Moore
Body　Claret floss, ribbed oval gold
Wing　Magenta bucktail with black bucktail over

Skunk Tail
Body　Black floss, ribbed oval silver
Wing　Blue bucktail with skunk tail outside

Stewart's Killer
Body　Silver tinsel, ribbed oval
Wing　Red squirrel with black squirrel outside

Sweep
Body　Black floss, ribbed oval gold
Wing　Black squirrel
Hackle　Blue cock dressed as collar

Willie Gunn
Body　Black floss, ribbed oval gold
Wing　Orange-yellow-black bucktail mixed

The tube and Waddington fly patterns listed can be interchanged as can some of the traditional and hairwing dressings, thus giving a range of patterns for salmon fishing that will meet almost every fishing situation. However there are some anglers who wish to retain the very effective hooking capability of the treble hook without the body bulk of the tube or the length of the Waddington shank. They require a lightly dressed, short, slim fly with the holding capabilities that only a treble hook can provide. To meet this specification a longer shank treble hook with loop-eye and needle sharp points has been designed, known as the E. D. (Esmond Drury) fly treble hook. It has gained a reputation for effective hooking with more fish being landed in relation to the number of offers. Also, with the loop-eye the turtle knot can be used although I much prefer to use the grinner knot which was devised by the late Richard Walker.

E. D. Treble Hook Flies

My next series of flies are designed for E. D. treble hooks. The hairwings, as in the previous patterns, are dressed so that they encircle the hookshank; if a hackle is required for the dressing, tie it in front of the wing and wind as a collar, then sweep it back and overtie.

April Flasher (*Plate 18*)
Tail   Red wool
Body   Black wool, ribbed silver oval
Wing   Orange calf hair mixed red Flashabou

Black Flasher (*Plate 18*)
Tail   D.F.M. lime green wool
Body   Black floss, ribbed silver oval
Wing   Black squirrel mixed silver Flashabou

Blue Flasher (*Plate 18*)
Tail   Blue wool
Body   Silver tinsel, ribbed oval
Wing   White calf hair mixed blue Flashabou

Claret Flasher (*Plate 18*)
Tail   Claret wool
Body   Copper tinsel, ribbed copper wire
Wing   Claret calf hair mixed red Flashabou

Golden Flasher (*Plate 18*)
Tail   Golden-yellow wool
Body   Gold tinsel, ribbed oval
Wing   Brown calf tail mixed gold Flashabou
Hackle   Long fibred dyed lemon-yellow cock

Goat's Foot (*Plate 18*)
Tail   Red wool
Body   Peacock herl
Hackle   Blue peacock neck

June Flasher
Tail   D.F.M. green wool
Body   Peacock herl, ribbed yellow floss
Wing   Yellow, brown calf hair mixed red and blue Flashabou

Logie
Tag   Yellow floss
Body   Red floss, ribbed silver oval
Wing   Yellow and red calf hair mixed blue Flashabou

Magenta Flasher
Tail   D.F.M. magenta wool
Body   Black wool, ribbed silver oval
Wing   Black squirrel mixed red and silver Flashabou

Red Flasher
Tail   Red wool
Body   Gold tinsel, ribbed red floss
Wing   Brown calf hair mixed red Flashabou

Red Abbey
Tail   Red wool
Body   Red floss, ribbed gold oval
Wing   Brown squirrel mixed gold Flashabou

Orange Flasher
Tail   D.F.M. orange wool
Body   Gold tinsel, ribbed oval
Wing   Orange calf hair mixed gold Flashabou
Hackle   Black cock

White Flasher
Tail   Pink wool
Body   D.F.M. white wool, ribbed silver oval
Wing   White calf hair mixed red Flashabou
Hackle   Badger cock

The wool tails should be tied in short so that the cut edge of the wool just protrudes beyond the hook bend. If dressing a pattern that requires both hairwing and hackle, the hair must be dressed very sparsely. The E. D. hook (treble) is most effective sparsely dressed; overdressing must be avoided.

Shrimps and Prawns

There are not many patterns that effectively imitate the prawn or shrimp. The most well known dressings are Curry's Golden Shrimp and Red Shrimp plus the famous General Practitioner, a prawn imitation devised by Esmond Drury in the 1950s. I have devised patterns which in my view are just as effective and considerably cheaper to produce as they do not require the expensive jungle cock and golden pheasant plumage; also my dressings can be tied a lot more quickly. I tie my patterns on 1/0 single loop-eyed hooks with a size ten flying treble hook on nylon line about 4 cm (1¹/₂ in) from the 1/0 hookbend.

My prawn dressings are not difficult to tie and I hope the following instruction will suffice. I use foam rubber of the type that is normally used for padding cushions for the bodies; it is available in most colours and with a sharp pair of scissors it is easy to cut off narrow strips for winding the bodies. Prepare the flying treble mount as instructions given on page 21.

To tie the prawn, first wind the silk down the body of the hookshank, tie in a strip of foam and wind and then secure. This has increased the diameter of the hookshank. Now tie the bucktail encircling the foam body with the fine hair points veiling the flying treble hook. Bind the loose bucktail down on the body foam, trimming off any surplus hair out over the hookeye. Tie in the latex or foam back – then tie in gold ribbing and another strip of foam rubber. Wind the foam to form a prawn-shaped body and then rib it with the oval tinsel.

Tie in hackle and wind, sweep the hackle back and overtie it and bring the latex or foam backing over the top and tie in. Form the head and trim the surplus material pointing out over the hookeye so as to form the prawn's feet, rather like a pair of seal's flippers. Do not make them too big or they will impart too much spin to the fly and cause kinking in the cast. When winding the gold rib you will notice that the ribbing will almost disappear into the body foam. Don't take any notice of this; the soft lifelike feeling this foam rubber imparts to the body I am sure encourages the fish to hold on to the fly.

Orange Prawn
Tail   Orange bucktail
Body   Orange foam, ribbed gold oval
Back   Orange foam or latex
Hackle   Long fibred hot orange cock saddle
Tying Silk   Red or orange

Red Prawn
Tail   Orange or red bucktail
Body   Red foam, ribbed gold oval
Back   Red foam or latex
Hackle   Natural red cock saddle
Tying silk   Red

Brown Prawn
Tail   Light brown bucktail dyed orange
Body   Off-white foam, ribbed gold oval
Back   Natural latex
Hackle   Natural red cock saddle
Tying silk   Grey

My prawn patterns can be dressed on to a tube. I use the clear flexible plastic tubing similar to the type used for car windscreen washer systems. This tubing has thicker walls and larger inside diameter which helps to make a fat-looking prawn. Place the tube on the eyeless salmon hookshank and wind on the silk. It is important the prawn fishes the right way up: to achieve this tie a very narrow strip of lead which will be the belly of the prawn. Now tie in a underbelly of foam; having done this complete the tube in the same mode as the previous instructions. When using a prawn dressed on a flexible tube, particularly when you are fishing the water and just letting the artificial swing around in the current, it pays to bend the tube just a little out of alignment as this will cause the artificial to move about. However, if you bend it too much, the spin will be too great and you will have to tie in a swivel on the leader.

Rubber Worm Fly
Hook   1/0 with size 10 flying treble
Legs   Brown rubber bands cut in half
Body   Brown foam with peacock herl over

Tie in an underbody of foam on the 1/0 hook, then tie in a bunch of rubber bands trimmed to a length just long enough to mask the flying treble. Tie in peacock herl and wind to cover the foam underbody. This dressing should now look rather like a squid or a bunch of worms, depending a little on your view point. On its day the rubber band worm fly can be very effective indeed; it is best fished using a fast sinking line and a very short leader of 1.25–1.60 m (4–5 ft).

   This pattern can also be tied on a tube; there is no need to use lead as it does not matter which way up the fly swims. Keep the tube short, using the clear plastic screenwasher tubing. Cut a piece about 2.5 cm (1 in) in length, this will do nicely for the head. Use a tulip to set the treblehook off from the tube and also to keep it in line. For the flying treble on my prawn and worm fly dressings I like to use the E. D. treble.

Bootlace
Hook   Size 1 loop-eyed single
Body   Grey/black large rubber band cut in half

Hackle   Iron blue dun
Tying silk   Dark grey

A very simple dressing: bind the end of the rubber band onto the hookshank with about 10 cm (4 in) projecting out over the hookbend. Tie in the hackle, winding it then sweeping it back so that it envelops the hookshank, overtie and complete the head. This fly at times can be a useful addition to the flyfisher's tactics as it is quite a good imitation of the elver.

11

Feathers of Game and Other Birds

Every feather on any bird can be utilised in one form or other for dressing flies. In this chapter I list the more widely used feathers in the bird's plumage so that the reader can relate them more effectively to the fly patterns. Water-based birds such as duck, goose, coot and moorhen provide a whole range of feathers and quills to enable the fly-tyer to practise his craft. The mallard, particularly the drake, provides a wide selection of suitable plumage starting with the brown or bronze shoulders. The blue and grey wing quills are good for winging, particularly the grey wing quills which are excellent for double split dry fly wings. The grey flank feathers are used for sea trout and salmon fly wings and the smaller sizes for fan wings for mayfly imitations. The teal is probably best known for its grey and black barred flank feathers which are used for winging famous trout and sea trout patterns like the Teal and Blue, Teal and Red and Peter Ross which are known worldwide.

A wide range of wet flies can be dressed with the dark blue dun and iron dun hackles from the coot and moorhen. Their wing quills provide the right colour feathers for the wings of many patterns and the small feathers from the inside of the wing near the elbow are very useful for spider patterns.

The white goose provides a whole range of feathers, particularly for the salmon fly dresser who requires a wide range of dyed colours for his patterns. The large quills and shoulder stiffs are used mainly in the large built wings that are tied on 2/0 hooks and above. The goose shoulder feathers are rather softer and marry much better than the quills and stiffs, and are used in the main for the fully dressed salmon fly patterns. Some of the old patterns give swan shoulder or quills for the wings: swan is a protected species, so for the modern tyer goose is the swan substitute. Goose cossette are smaller body feathers, very easy to marry and can be used for the built wings of small salmon flies and sea trout flies. The cossette, dyed bright red, is an ideal substitute for ibis and can be used for trout fly tails such as the Butcher and Alexandra. Wild grey geese, the pinkfoot and the greyleg, provide herls for the bodies of flies such as the Grey Goose nymph and dry flies like the Grey Duster. Many of the body feathers will make ideal wings for spent fly patterns and they can be trimmed to any size. If you use a wing-cutting tool it is possible to produce perfect spent dry fly wings.

Kingfishers and herons are protected in the United Kingdom, however there is still plumage available which are the remnants of the millinery trade. The blue hackles of the kingfisher can be used in place of blue chatterer as cheeks in salmon fly patterns – very often they are tied in over the jungle cock eyes. Heron quills and shoulders are useful for wings and herls. The long flowing hackles makes superb flies; they are soft and mobile, imparting such vitality to the fly that fish cannot resist having a go at it.

Birds of the wetlands, snipe and woodcock, provide some useful hackles; snipe hackles are used in the sparsely-dressed north country patterns. The woodcock quill is used for providing wings for the woodcock series of flies. I like to use the woodcock hackle with dubbed seal's fur bodies ribbed with wide oval tinsel and find this type of dressing very effective for lake trout.

The grey partridge is another useful source of hackles, the brown and grey feathers being used for the very popular partridge series of flies. I particularly like the grey hackle, especially the very light coloured as it is easy to dye a bright colour. To dye just a few hackles, I select them for size, choosing the pale coloured ones and pull off the fluffy fibres at the base of the hackle. I wash them in warm soapy water to remove any grease in the feathers so that the dye will take. The dye can be prepared in a saucer of hot water with a drop of vinegar as a colour fixer. Holding them by the stalk, I dip each hackle into the bath and swish it about so that the dye is absorbed into the feather fibres. This method of dyeing ensures the colour is controlled, for each feather can be dyed light or dark depending on the time it is in the bath. Lightly dyed hackles certainly improve some flies, for an example a lightly dyed grey partridge hackle in place of the natural hackle on a traditional partridge pattern makes for a superb looking fly and fish catcher.

The French partridge, also known as the redleg, does not have the same flytying range of feathers as the grey; however its breast feathers are used for fan wings and winging some mayfly patterns.

The common pheasant attains adult plumage in its first year. These pheasant are reared and released in large numbers on sporting estates. The plumage of the common pheasant is variable, from the distinct white ring on the neck type to the dark melanistic. There is hardly a feather on a normal coloured pheasant that cannot be utilized by the fly-tyer. On a typical cock bird, its plumage starting from his head has the following colours: blue neck, gold sides, reddish brown shoulders and breast, (usually these feathers are edged with black), short green rump, light brown wing quills with brown centre and side tail feathers. The speckled plumage of the hen bird is useful; this can range in colour from a pale cream cinnamon right through to a charcoal shade. The wing quills and tail feathers are suitable for winging flies like the Invicta, March Brown etc.

The Japanese green pheasant plumage is a blue-green/black neck, bronze-green sides, blue-black or blue-green shoulders and breast. It has green-blue rump feathers and the tail feathers have grey and dark blue bars. There is not much to choose colourwise between the melanistic and green pheasant.

Overall the common pheasant is a most versatile source of materials for the tyer and the cheapest way to buy pheasant feathers is to go to your nearest shoot after a day's shooting and buy a brace of pheasants and skin them (*see Chapter 14*).

Grouse speckled tails and hackles are used on the grouse series of flies and there is no reason why they cannot be used on any pattern that requires a dark hackle in its dressing.

Guinea fowls are not game birds in the true sense, but some keepers release a few with their pheasants to act as watchdogs as their alarm calls soon lets him know if there is anything or anybody near the release pen. If on a shoot day one of the guns shoots one by mistake they are usually required to pay a penalty for their error. Guinea fowl tails and wing quills are used in a great many fully dressed salmon flies. Their hackles are in great demand, dyed or natural, in salmon flies and lures;

in the large salmon flies they are dyed blue as a substitute for the blue jay wing quill feather.

There are many birds with coloured and exotic plumage that the fly-dresser can use in his craft. The two most beautiful and popular of the entire pheasant family for the fly tyer are the golden pheasant and Lady Amherst pheasant. They are known as ruffed pheasants because of their beautiful tippet neck colour and they do not attain their full adult plumage until their second year. They are the only two species in this group, and will interbreed quite freely, producing some very colourful crosses. All the hybrids are fertile and endless colours have been produced, some of them very beautiful indeed, although the splendour of the original parents has never really been surpassed.

The plumage of the golden pheasant is very beautiful and the following description is as accurate as it is possible to give. It is very difficult to describe its plumage fully and I hope my attempt will give some idea of the beauty and splendour of this magnificent bird. On the crown of the head is the topping crest of elongated golden yellow feathers. The tippet collar is formed of broad rectangular feathers, the visible part of which is orange in colour with two black-blue bars across it. The breast is scarlet merging into light chestnut in the middle of the abdomen and thighs. The upper part of the back is covered with dark green rectangular feathers and the rump feathers are a deep yellow merging into brown. The wing quills are brown and the tail feathers are mottled black and brown. The principle feathers used by the fly-tyer are the toppings and tippets for tails or wings, red breast and yellow rump feathers for hackles and wings. Tail feathers are used in the main for built wings and are also useful for nymphs, tail and horns.

There is a prawn dressing for salmon which, apart from the dyed hot orange seal's fur and gold oval tinsel, is completely dressed with the plumage of the golden pheasant and very effective it is too.

The plumage of the golden pheasant hen is in the main medium to dark brown with a suggestion of a yellowish tint in the whole effect. When incubating the hen is a faithful broody, rarely leaving the nest for food and water, and when the chicks are hatched proves to be quite a capable mother.

The golden pheasant cock is sensitive to sunlight which discolours the golden toppings to almost a pale washy yellow, also the orange tippet will be affected. To prevent this happening, after the bird has moulted into its bright new plumage keep it out of the sun as much as possible during the summer months.

Two more varieties of the golden pheasant exist: the dark golden pheasant and the yellow golden pheasant. These varieties appear to be the results of a mutation, not cross-breeding.

The Lady Amherst pheasant was introduced into Britain by Lord Amherst; after a few more importations with some ups and downs the species became established. The Lady Amherst adapted to aviary conditions and, breeding very successfully, soon increased its numbers. It is however a pity that more males were imported than females, resulting in the males being cross-bred with golden pheasant hens. This continuous practice over the years has produced a large number of hybrid Amherst pheasants and a pure Lady Amherst is a pretty rare bird. To identify golden pheasant strain in a Lady Amherst's cock look for the following characteristics: red colour on the flanks and thighs, scarlet instead of orange tips in the tail coverts, traces of the mottled effect on the tail feathers, a crest that is too big.

To enable the reader to recognise the gorgeous Lady Amherst's pheasant cock, here is a brief description. On the crown of its head are short green feathers followed by topping crest of elongated crimson feathers and a tippet collar of rounded white feathers edged with blue black at the tips. It has a black-bluish green back with yellow rump, tail-feathers grey-white with black bars.

The Lady Amherst's hen pheasant is very similar to the golden pheasant but larger. The tail feathers are rounded not pointed as the golden.

There are a few salmon fly patterns that use Amherst pheasant plumage in their dressings. I believe there is a fully dressed salmon fly that goes by the name of Lady Amherst.

The plumage of the silver pheasant is sometimes used by the fly-dresser so I include a short description of this attractive bird, particularly the male with his long tail feathers. The upper body of the cock has a white colour with narrow black lines running across. The crest and underbody are a dark blue. The side tails are barred black and white with the centre tails pure white. This pheasant, like the golden and Lady Amherst, does not attain full adult plumage until the second year of its life; all the descriptions relate only to matured birds.

Peafowl are a most useful producer of feathers for the fly-dresser; starting from the head it provides the tyer with this magnificent range of feathers: blue neck feathers followed by the green body feathers, with the gold back feathers and the sword and eye feathers from which we get our herls and quills, plus the wing quills for flies. Their large size and long colourful feathers gives the peafowl a most impressive appearance. Their needs are simple if they are able to free range; they will find a large portion of their food and a few handfuls of mixed corn daily should complete their needs.

The two main species are the Indian and the green peafowl. They will cross-breed freely producing a completely fertile hybrid. There is the black shoulder peacock which is a mutation from the Indian peafowl; this mutation is truly a magnificent example of the peafowl, which on the whole are fairly hardy and reasonably easy to breed. They do not acquire their full adult plumage until their third year.

Ostrich plumes supply the herl which have many varied applications from the bodies for nymphs to the butts of salmon flies. The long fibred fluffy soft herl makes perfect translucent bodies for nymphs particularly if they are ribbed with tinsel.

Jungle fowls are part of the pheasant family and are only found in the wild state in the eastern part of the world. There are four species of jungle fowl; the red jungle fowl, the grey, the green and the Ceylon species. The jungle fowl which is of most interest to the flydresser is the grey or Sonnerat's jungle fowl. It is the grey jungle cock which gives the fly-tyer that beautiful yellow chrome shiny-eyed hackle feather that is used for cheeks or eyes for many sea trout and salmon fly patterns. This chrome eyed hackle is most unusual and the Sonnerat's jungle fowl cock is the only fowl in the world to have it – it is not unusual to have white spangles on the end of hackles in poultry but not where the feather has fused together to form two shiny solid plates. At the tip the eye is shiny – yellow chrome and a smaller more white solid eye below it about quarter of the way down the hackle. It takes two years for the jungle cock to attain adult plumage and in its first year the plates tend to be white. The saddle hackles can be used for lures and the

Plate 17: Salmon Hair Wing Flies (see Chapter 9)

Trudie	Wendy	Gwendoline
Black Tamish	Orange Tamish	Red/Orange Tamish
Jungle Stoat	Silver Dart	Black Dart
Camel's Tail	Cosseboom	Goldie
Willie Gunn	Logie	Yellow Torrish

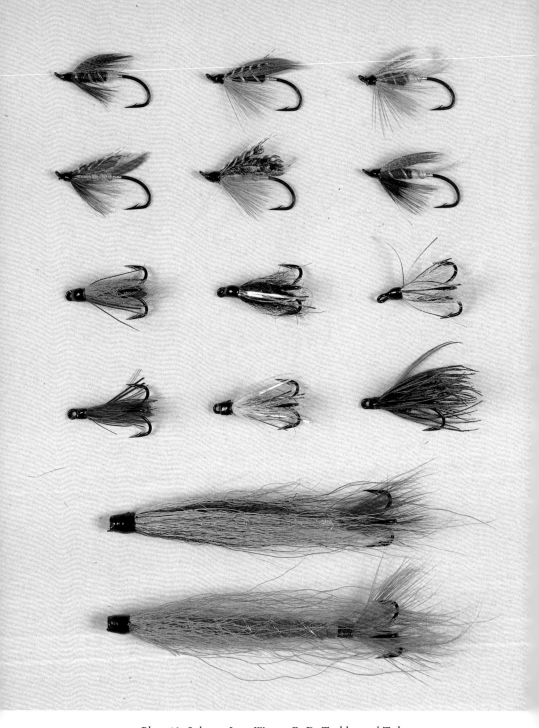

Plate 18: Salmon Low Water. E. D. Trebles and Tubes

Low Water (see Chapter 9):
Claret Alder
Skirmisher

E.D. Trebles (see Chapter 10):
April Flasher
Claret Flasher

Blue Charm
Sir Charles

Black Flasher
Golden Flasher

Logie
Jockie

Blue Flasher
Goat's Foot

Tubes (see Chapter 10):
Blue and Silver Tube
Orange Tube

Plate 19: Hackles

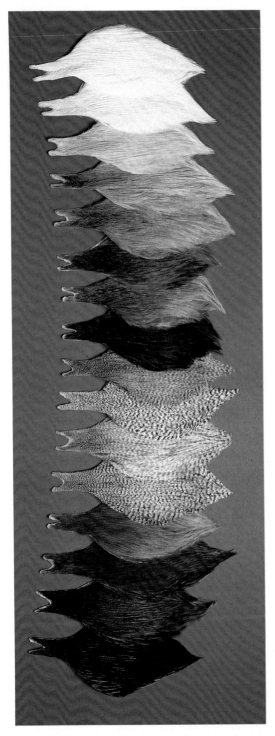

White

Cream

Watery Blue Dun

Light Blue Dun

Medium Blue Dun

Dark Blue Dun

Rusty Blue Dun

Bronze Blue Dun

Dun Grizzly

Grizzly

Ginger Variant

Cree

Ginger

Brown

Furnace

Black

Plate 20: Colorado Quality Hackles: Colours

centre white list can be coloured with felt pens; some very interesting combinations can be devised. I find the eyed feather invaluable for using in fully dressed salmon flies I am tying to go into frames; the jungle cock eye really completes the dressing and looks good behind glass.

In recent years there have been a few people trying to breed grey jungle fowl commercially for the fly-tying trade. I believe breeding problems have been quite considerable: poor hatching, low rate of chick survival and disease in the breeding stock. The one or two people who are still in business have largely solved these difficulties and are now producing jungle cock eyes for the fly-tyer. The hackles in the main are plucked from the bird's each year with the odd cape becoming available.

A useful source of material comes from the plumage of birds which are normally classified as pests in the United Kingdom: the crow, pigeon, jay, rook and jackdaw. Their hackles can be used in all types of patterns from lightweight spiders to the heavy tubes for salmon fishing; there are a good selection of soft hackles to be found underneath the wings. If a tyer is looking for mobile soft hackles probably the best ones are found under the wings regardless of species.

The turkey is the source of the soft marabou feather and the wing quills and rump feathers make good herls. They are very useful for lures and salmon fly wings. Turkey colours will range from white to black and they can be found in virtually any colour and shade, although some shades of colour are now rare, which also applies to some turkey breeds.

12

Hackles – Quality, Age and Shape

Angling writers over the past 130 years or so have written that only oldish cocks produce quality hackles, but they have never produced evidence to support this assertion. It would appear this is one of those nice sayings which has been passed down over the years without anybody ever bothering to check its validity. What they should have said is that quality hackles are only obtained from matured cocks; once a bird has attained its adult plumage, at eight to ten months old depending on the breed, the quality will not improve.

In my experience a cock needs to be a year old to acquire that bloom which makes its hackles most attractive, but the quality of its hackles at this age will be its quality for life, and I have kept cocks up to five years old, plucking hackles for fly-tying from them each year. There is no doubt that immature cockerel hackles are soft until the final moult into adult plumage, so perhaps this is what the writers of the past were trying to warn against. In 1975 I exchanged considerable correspondence with the late H. F. D. Elder on this subject and we were in complete agreement on age and quality. In February 1976 the *Trout and Salmon* magazine published an article of mine in which I reported in full my experiences regarding age and colours of hackles. The article passed without comment from the readers, so it would appear that nobody has any evidence to the contrary. It is, I suppose, physically possible that some strains of poultry may require up to two years to acquire their adult plumage (like some species of pheasants), but nobody as yet has produced any evidence to support this.

In 1987 I was in touch regarding hackles and breeding with a renowned poultry expert who consults worldwide on avian diseases and nutrition, Dr Carey L. Quarles of Colorado Quality Hackles, Fort Collins, USA, and he confirmed that Colorado Hackles harvest their cocks at about ten months old. By using a computer for their programme they ensure their grades usually run 87 per cent No 1 and No 2 capes. He makes the point that he selects for early maturity and there are also certain nutritional items that can aid feather development which explains why his percentage is so good. Stiffness of hackles is hereditary, and another hereditary factor is that some chickens start feathering earlier than others and the breeder must take advantage of this. Selecting only from these birds for breeding, it is possible to produce a strain of early-feathering birds that acquire their adult plumage sooner, thus cutting down the time for producing hackles. Dr Quarles has obviously taken advantage of this fact, and by using the computer has reaped the full benefit.

A hackle of any quality should, when held by the stalk and bent over, then released, flick back like a spring, or when you shake it vigorously and suddenly stop, it should quiver like a jelly. Look for a lance shape; barbs (fibres) of even length from bottom to top of the hackles, with barbs short and even each side of the hackle stalk. The colour on the reverse side of the hackles should be good with no or little web. For the bi-colours look for a clear cut centre list; with barred hackles, make sure the barring is clear and defined; for quality, the colours must not merge or run into each other. Quality hackle colours must have plenty of sparkle and sheen when twisted round in the light.

To test the stiffness of the individual barbs, wind the hackle on to a hookshank. The barb should be relatively thick and short which gives a stiff barb capable of supporting the fly. A dodge fly-tyers use when they have a hackle too large for the dry fly they are tying is simply to trim the barb to size – not good fly-tying practice but it enables full use of a cape of good quality and colour.

The only thing that may change with age in some birds is their colour, so perhaps this is what the writers of the past and present mean when they say 'Hackles improve with age'. Some of my barred Plymouth Rocks during the summer months take on a yellow tint on the grey-white bars of their plumage which I think makes the hackles most attractive, but after the moult the birds are back to their normal colour. I have plucked these hackles and tied them into flies and they retain this yellow tint even after plenty of use.

I do not agree with many angling writers who express the view that hackle stiffness is more important than colour, as it is my belief that, providing the stiffness is adequate, colour is the most important factor. Too many times I have had flies ignored by trout until I have changed to another of the same pattern but with a slightly differently coloured hackles. Two very effective variations I devised of R. S. Austin's Blue Upright are tied with a barred blue hackle or a barred yellowish hackle. Fishing these two variations dry on a small moorland stream one afternoon some twenty odd years ago I rose and hooked over sixty trout of which twelve were large enough to keep.

The shape and quality of hen hackles are as important for quality wet flies as they are for the cock hackles for dry flies and present the same problems of selection. It is no good trying to tie flies with hen hackles that are so heavily webbed that it is impossible to wind them; the barbs will cling together while being wound so instead of neatly tied fly with the hackles barbs splayed around the hookshank, there will be a horrible spikey hackle with four or five lots of hackle fibres all stuck together. I prefer hen hackles that are finger-shaped and rounded at the tip like a point of a teaspoon. With experience it is not difficult to recognise hackles that are too heavily webbed and of no use to the fly-tyer.

The basic colours of hen hackles are the same as the cocks, except the red is more orange or yellow. I have seen orange red in hens but never the deep red that you see in the cocks. Some of the hen hackle markings are very beautiful, particularly the hackles that are laced or edged with a different colour. I have seen very dark blue hen capes where the hackles have flecks or spots of other colours in their makeup; my favourite hackle is where the colour starts light coloured in the centre and progressively becomes darker towards the edge.

My ideal hackle shape is long and narrow, with even barb length from top to bottom. What does this description mean? Short in the barb, long in length? What does it mean by short, and how long is long? John Henderson published a simple and reliable way of judging a hackle for size in the *Fly Fisher's Journal* in 1932. This method of measurement works as follows:

a Total hackle length 8.0 cm
b Useful hackle length 6.0 cm
c Barb length 1.3 cm

The *useful length* of the hackle is what is left after the soft downy fibres at the base of the hackle have been removed to allow for the tip to be held in hackle pliers. Therefore a useful length of 6.0 cm divided into a barb length of 1.3 cm will give a hackle ratio of 4.6/1.0, using the formula

Useful length ÷ barb = ratio.

This ratio can only refer to hackles of a size normally used for dry flies; obviously the ratio improves in the larger hackle sizes.

A useful guide to *barb length* in relation to hook sizes, assuming the hackle length is adequate, is:

Barb Length	Hook Size (Redditch)
0.4 – 0.5 cm	20 – 16
0.6 – 0.8 cm	16 – 14
1.0 cm	14 – 12
1.1 – 1.3 cm	12 – 10

Any hackle ratio over 4/1 refers to a hackle which is top class. However this only applies to hackles suitable for normal dry flies up to size ten Redditch scale.

The ratio for useful hackle length to barb length which I consider to be the ideal hackle in the dry fly size is 5/1. I found this virtually impossible to achieve in my Old English game fowl, however in my barred Plymouth Rocks I have consistently matched this standard and very often surpassed it. The saddle hackles have very short barbs in relation to their length, and I could dress two or three flies with just one hackle or a complete palmer bodied dry fly. The hackle length to barb length ratio with my barred saddle hackles could go as high as 14/1. The average was in the region of 10/1, the barb length varying between 0.4 cm and 0.8 cm, the useful length between 4.0 cm and 10.0 cm.

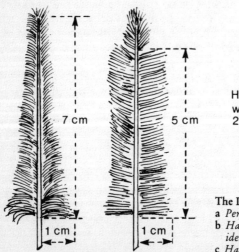 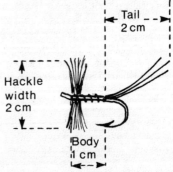

The Ideal Hackle Ratio 5/1
a *Perfect hackle shape, length 7 cm, barb 1 cm*
b *Hackle spread ready for tying in, showing the ideal hackle ratio of 5/1*
c *Hackle tied into fly*

In the diagram above, the fly dimensions are:
Hook   Size 12 wide gape
Tail fibres length   2 cm
Body length   1 cm
Barb length   1 cm
Hackle width   2 cm

The acquisition of a cape loaded with hackles in the 5/1 ratio would be most unlikely. However, a top quality cape should have plenty of hackles in the dry fly sizes to a ratio of 3.8/1. When using capes that are of a lower grade you can always trim your hackles to size, assuming the stiffness is adequate.

There are various types of poorly shaped hackles that are not easily spotted; some hackles have barbs at the base of the shaft which are longer than the ones further up, or sometimes the barbs are longer further up the stalk than they are at the base. I have seen hackles that, when spread, have barbs of normal length except that every third or fourth barb is longer with a very fine tip which runs or lies on the edge of the hackle, looking towards the hackle tip. This condition varies quite considerably, sometimes it is every barb on the hackle that has a fine hair-like tip or only just a few have them. It is reasonably easy to pick out a hackle where all the barbs have these fine hair-like tips, because this condition produces a thin, darker colour on the edge of the hackle. In hackles where there are only a few of the barbs affected, the only way to discover this condition is to spread the hackles out.

Carey Quarles of Colorado Hackles sent me sample hackles from his breeders 1987 (cocks) and invited my evaluation of them. The most outstanding feature of them was their shape. I have never before seen such ideal shapes through such a wide range of colours. The colours were white, cream, furnace, brown, black and blue and most of them were to my ideal hackle standard – some of them were even better which was quite remarkable. The overall quality was very good, the whites and creams a little softer than the rest, but when you consider the general standard of white and cream hackles these Colorado feathers are in a class of their own. I can only think of one word to describe these hackles in all the colours – superb.

H. C. Cunliffe gives an interesting account of hackles in his book *The Art of Trout Fishing on Rapid Streams*, published in 1863. I quote from him extensively below as all he wrote is still largely relative today as regards to hackles, though I disagree with his description of a quality hackle shape.

Of hackles Cutcliffe writes: 'And now we must speak of hackles – which are very various in description and colour; and as of all the parts of a fly the hackle is the most important, much attention and care should be bestowed upon the selection and collection of these feathers. Many hackles may be obtained of good colour, but indifferent shape, or good shape and bad colour or a colour which though good when out of the water is bad when immersed in it. A hackle then should be of a brilliant lustre, reflecting and sparkling in the light, when moved about in the finger; if the colour of the shining part of the hackle be red, the root or that part nearest the insertion of the feather should be black or nearly so, and the under side of the feather should be dark; also, if blue, (or what fishermen calls blue, the natural living colours of such feathers) the root should be nearly black, (a little down will always be found close to the root of the feather, this must always be pulled off, as it does not form a part of what the fisherman terms the hackle – it seems an appendage, or perhaps young and undeveloped fibres) in fact in all feathers, excepting very light blues, the root should be the darkest part of the hackle. In dark hackles the tip and extreme edges of the fibres forming the feathers, should be darker than the centre. All hackles should be plucked from a cock's neck; hen's hackles are worse than useless in rapid streams; they have no stiffness, cannot resist the force of the water washing on them; and consequently lie flat along the hook, lose all the little colour they have when dry, and make your fly hook more like a little oval black mass of dirt, rather than a living insect; a few fish would attempt so uninviting a morsel as this represents. The shape of the feather should be an isosceles triangle, having its base at the end which is inserted into the skin, and its alongated apex, slenderly, gradually, and evenly tapering off to a fine point – many will be found suddenly ending in a rounded extremity these are not so good, but some of them if of fine colour may be retained. Then the hackle must be stiff and elastic, the fibres standing out indepedently and bodily from the midrib or stalk of the feather, like so many bristles set each at exactly the same angle. A common mode of trying or examining a hackle, is after pulling or stripping of the down at the root, to take it by the stem and with the bright side upwards, place it on the sleeve of a coat, if black, or on any dark object, when the brilliant lustre of the feather will be displayed and then by pressing the apex against the cloth, bend it, by which we judge of its shape, the regularity of tapering of the fibres, and its stiffness and elasticity in regaining its natural shape, after being impressed and bent in any direction.

'The best of all fowls for hackles is the Old English Game cock, which, however is now very difficult to be obtained, no bird seems to have such lustrous, shining, stiff and well-shaped feathers as this game fowl, such as was used in times of yore for cock fighting; if these cannot be procured, anyone wishing to keep a stock of fowls for feathers, will do well to purchase a blue hen from a farm yard, where most of the fowls are either blue or red and black, where indeed the breed seems especially of a blue-red or blackish colour, and mate this hen with a well bred dark-red or black-red bantam cock; the chicken will be of a small size, but one of the cocks a dark colour (blue or red) should be mated with a hen similar to the parent hen, all the others being destroyed, and from this generation we may perpetuate a class of fowls very similar to the old game fowl; the cross with the bantam fines down the feather, makes it more delicate better shaped, and brighter in colour; and from this stock of fowls, red, blues, and black will alone be born. By choosing a red bantam we shall ensure a richness of tinge in our hackle, and procure more rusty blue and reds than plain and sober coloured feathers. These rusty feathers are by far the most rare, and by far the best when obtained; they combine several colours, and shot as it were over the surface of a rich glossy grounding in blue and red, and on scrutinizing their surface carefully we perceive the exact similarity in tints of shading to the natural colour of various furs, as the ends of hare's flax, water rat, and mouse and fox fur, pulled our and mixed well together.'

Continuing, Cutcliffe goes on to say of his birds: 'I generally pluck my fowls twice in the year, in the spring as soon as the bird has assumed his gay summer dress, and again, late in the autumn before moulting season, when I find many hackles which in the spring I would not take, because too small, now however grown of proper size.'

13

Breeding for Colour, Quality and Shape

When I started breeding for hackles at the beginning of 1960 there was very little information available on what types of poultry were suitable for hackle production. My intention was to produce blue duns; at that time the colour was so uncommon that to acquire any shade of blue dun cape with quality dry fly hackles was virtually impossible at any price. (Even now, although quality blue dun capes are being specially bred for the fly-tyer, they are still quite expensive.) I decided, colour would be my first priority when breeding, followed by quality. My most difficult problem was to find suitable breeding stock; most poultry was being produced in intensive systems and there were very few free range systems being operated with the right types for my programme.

It was a marvellous piece of luck, therefore, that I was introduced to a breeder in Launceston who kept bantam barred Plymouth Rocks for showing and was very successful at local and national shows. The colour was superb and the quality reasonable – unfortunately he would not sell me any cocks of show standard and no barred hens but eventually I persuaded him to part with one light coloured barred cockerel and three black hens. He said that breeding the light coloured cock to black hens would produce some birds as good as some of the birds he had shown me. Also, if his cock's colour started to become too light he would breed back to the black hens to darken the colour. Within the two years I was breeding barred rocks as good as his, even hatching out a few barred hens. I ran the black and barred hens as a flock to keep the dark clear colour in the cocks.

The barred Plymouth Rock is an interesting breed which first came into being in America around 1860. There was an earlier bird called Plymouth Rock but it had reddish barred hackles and feathered legs and feet. I do not know exactly what breeds were crossed to produce the Barred Rock as we know it, but I have traced two breeds that, so it was said, were part of the original cross breeding. The first is the Black Java; this colour often throws back in the modern bird on the female side, so if you hatch out black hens it shows that your strain is true to the original breeding. The second breed, or rather type, is the Dominique (the American term for cuckoo or blue barred). For many years the Barred Rock was the leading breed in the United States which explains why so many flies with barred hackles in their dressings originate from there.

The American birds are on the whole somewhat lighter in colour than the British birds. The bars of the British bird's plumage are black and grey-white, the American birds are blue-white with dark blue bars which stops short of positive black, giving a distinctly blueish colour in the whole effect. Most of the British birds appears a greyish colour; if the light catches the plumage at the right angle they appear to be almost silver. My own birds were on the whole darker than the British Show Standard, but I was breeding for fly-tying not showing. The bars on my birds were blue-grey-white and black.

Later I was given a lead to some breeders who specialised in Old English game fowl; this was the break I was looking for and it set me on the way to producing the blue dun hackle. One of the difficulties I experienced was recognising the various colours and knowing the O. E. G. names for them; some were used when the breed was kept mainly for cock fighting and are still applicable. To appreciate the colours in O. E. G. it should be realised that the colour relates only to the male bird. Accordingly the breeder refers to his bird first by the breast colour, for an example, black red means a male bird with a black breast and his hackle and saddle a red colour.

To confuse the beginner even further some descriptions are not based on breast colour first, but colour of the wing. There are a group of O. E. G. called duckwings which have a steel-blue coloured band across the wing similar to a mallard wing; this appears to be the reason for the name. This group consist of Golden, Silver and Birchen Duckwing plus some other colours which makes it very difficult to understand. Add to all this are the fighting and other names such as Piles, Pole-cats, Spangles, Creoles, Birchen Yellow, Furnesses, Brassy Backed, Bronzes, Pheasant Reds and duns plus all the off-colours. It is not surprising that the newcomer can be somewhat confused. For the colours to be understood and recognised they have to be seen. The only way to do this quickly is to visit poultry shows and talk to the breeders.

The list of colours I give I consider to be the most relative to the fly-tyer, considering the tremendous range in the breed available. With all the colours there are various shades and hues. On the male birds the saddle and neck hackles tends to be brighter and this applies even to the self colours. The summary for the various colours is intended only as a general guide and there is bound to be some loss of accuracy. However the difference will be small, and in regard to the fly-tyers needs, I don't consider this to be important.

Self Colours

White Cock: pure white with deeper hue on hackle and saddle. **Hen:** pure white
White Splashed Cock: white with black splashes or marks (blue bred). **Hen:** same as male
Black Cock: dull black (blue bred). **Hen:** same as male
Jet Black Cock: purple green black (metallic sheen). **Hen:** same as male.
Blue Cock: Dark hackle (blue black) with breast and thighs a grey-blue. **Hen:** different shade of blue sometimes ticked or laced.
Black Breasted Black/Red Cock: hackle, shoulders and saddle a dark blood-red, remainder black. **Hen:** black with purple-green sheen, hackle ticked with dark red.
Black/Red Cock: hackle, shoulder, saddle and wing bays red – remainder of plumage black. **Hen:** a range of hackle colours from golden to orange – body plumage varies quite a lot in different shades.
Brown/Red Cock: orange or yellow hackle. **Hen:** Striped orange or yellow.
Grey Cock: hackle and shoulder silvery-grey. **Hen:** silver striped hackle.
Pile Cock: hackle bright red or yellow. **Hen:** yellow striped hackle.
Gingers, Cock: hackle ginger to yellow red. **Hen:** Hackle light ginger to golden yellow.
Spangles, Cock: similar to Black/Red but with white spangles evenly distributed, preferably one spangle the end of each feather.

Creoles: barred plumage, black and white or red and white
Off Colours (Various): Honey Dun; Yellow Dun; Golden Dun; Silver Dun; Red Dun; Splashed various shades.

The following colours are rare and I am listing them to save the newcomer a time-wasting search

Old English Game Rare Colours

Pure White; Jet Black; Black Breasted Black Reds; Brown Breasted Brown Reds; Creoles; Polecats; Birchen Yellow; Bronzes; Pheasant Reds.

None of the Old English Game varieties are common and you may have to crossbreed to acquire them which is what I did in my early days. One of the problems I had breeding poultry was the lack of space, consequently my annual production was small and it took longer to achieve results, particularly in the more difficult colours. I think the only way to establish a hackle colour is with a high-turnover breeding programme.

In my first attempt to recreate blue I used an O. E. G. Black/Red cock and Pile hens. I had some interesting colours, some noteable red and orange capes but no blue feathering anywhere in the plumage of birds from this cross.

For my next attempt I used an Andalusian cock with Pile and Partridge hens. Out of this cross I had birds with blue in their plumage, but no blue necks; there were some well marked dark honey duns, furnace and ginger reds necks and saddles. The hackle quality and shape was so disappointing that I did not continue with them. Although the Andalusian is a soft feathered breed, I had hoped that crossing with Old English Game would have given quality of acceptable standard. (Incidently some writers give the appellation 'Andalusian' to any bird that has blue in its plumage and this is likely to confuse the novice.) The Andalusian is a breed that originally came from the Mediterranean area and the earliest recorded importation into England was 1851.

When I had all but given up trying to recreate blues, I acquired an O. E. G. Blue hen. Crossing this hen with an O. E. G. Black/Red cock gave some Blue Breasted Red cocks and Blue tailed hens which had well marked honey dun necks. Breeding the best Blue Breasted Red cock to the Blue hen the following season gave me some very interesting birds and hackles, but most important, I was on the way with my own strain of blues. I found the pure blues I was producing were a little too dark, particularly the male bird and some were virtually black, but breeding only from the 'splashed' birds ensured that the blue was from light to medium dark blue plus the other colours that always turn up when cross-breeding.

The Creole in Old English Game is a colour I have never seen and, out of interest I decided to recreate the barred red and white hackled bird. I crossed a Black/Red cock to barred Plymouth Rock hens. The results were variable had some interesting barred hackles. The next year I bred the best marked red and white barred cock to the barred hens and the hatching was a mixture of barred red and white, barred black and white, barred black, red and white with some plain colours. This cross held its colour over the years and after five years I was producing barred red and white birds.

Another useful cross I did was with a barred Plymouth Rock cock to Blue hens which produced some quite interesting and reasonably marked barred blues. The barring was not distinct enough with some birds but the range of colour was quite good. The following season I bred the hens of this cross back to the barred Plymouth Rock cock and the results were barred blue duns of a superb colour and acceptable quality. The only problem I had was the colour black coming through too strongly; half of each hatching was either black or very dark blue with a few lighter blue birds. The remainder were barred blue duns of various shades.

To breed a quality white cream hackle with a black list known (to fly-tyers) as a badger hackle, I would use a light Grey O. E. G. cock with as much list or dark centre in the hackle as possible. The hens should be splashed (blue bred) with as much white in the plumage as possible. Try to create enough breeding pens to fill a fifty-egg incubator weekly for a period of eight weeks; this should give a season hatch of over three hundred chicks. Once these birds have attained their adult plumage discard from the programme any bird that does not have a well marked list in a light coloured hackle. Hopefully there will be at least ten percent of the hatching with a well marked badger hackle suitable for the next season's breeding programme.

The second year, repeat the same programme, hatching out over three hundred chicks; there now should be a good percentage of this hatching with a well marked badger hackle. These birds will form the nucleus for the third year's programme; this year's breeding will give a high percentage of badger hackled birds, plus all the other colours which have been turning up each year, blues, honey duns of all shades and white or near whites. The white and near whites selectively bred together with some of the splashed birds will in a few years produce a strain of pure white; this can be done at the same time as the badger strain if the breeder has the space and time.

The furnace (red hackle with black list) can be produced by using this selective breeding technique; select a Black/Red cock with a well marked hackle; cross this cock with partridge hens of the black/red strain. It will take about three years to produce a true breeding strain of furnace hackled birds, but by careful selection it can be done.

Breeders with limited resources should concentrate on breeding barred Plymouth Rocks, O. E. G. black reds and the blues. These three types will provide all the hackle colours the fly-tyer breeder is likely to ever need.

Blue do not breed true (at least my strain never did), blue mated to blue gives a selection of blue, black and splashed chicks. Breeding Black (blue bred) to Black (blue bred) will produce a selection of dark blue to black with some lighter or splashed birds. Breeding splashed blue bred to splashed blue bred, selecting the white birds with only a little amount of dark blue or black marking on their plumage, will produce blue of all shades up to white. The near-white is a very creamy blue-white shade which when tied as spent wings gives the fly a translucency that needs to be seen to be appreciated. Black to Black and White to White will produce all the blacks and whites needed, but the quality may pose a few problems. To improve the quality of the black colour line and the white colour line in the second generation bring in different O. E. G. Black/Red cocks for each colour line. As well as improving the quality, it will put sparkle into the plumage. Breeding this way will give all sorts of off-colours but hopefully there will be enough black and white chicks to carry on the colour line.

To create a new blue strain, select a white or splashed cock from the black colour line and splashed hens from the white colour line. Cross these two blue bred colour lines and with selective breeding you will produce a new blue strain. This strain should not need fresh blood for some years; to lighten the colour it would be necessary for the first year, and perhaps the second, to breed only from the splashed birds. When the quality starts going back, bring in a good quality black/red cock to introduce hybrid vigour; everybody who breeds for hackles eventually realises the source of quality is the reds.

I do not know of any method of producing duns that guarantees success but by crossing black/red to blue a few honey duns, rusty duns and brassy duns may turn up – it is usually a hit and miss affair. Crossbreeding black/reds, blue/reds and blues will give such a wide range of blue dun shades and variations that it will be virtually impossible to find two blue dun capes which are exactly the same. In the blue dun, because of the black/red blood, there is often a reddish infusion in the hackle which gives a brassy rusty and gold colour on top of the blue. Twist the hackle in the light so that the light strikes it at an angle. The colour appears like gold dust sprinkled at random, extremely beautiful and gives a very realistic representation to a fly tied with such a hackle.

Frank Elder, in his *The Book of Hackle*, published in 1979, goes into hackle shape in considerable detail and I recommend anybody seriously considering breeding birds for hackles to acquire a copy. He gives a fascinating account of his work improving the hackle shape of his Old English Game fowl using a breed called Yokohama and the wild Red Jungle Fowl.

I was fortunate in that the hackle shape of my barred Plymouth Rocks was good, but I had to improve the strain to bring the stiffness up to the standard I required. However, in the Old English Game I started with, the shape was not good. The stiffness was adequate but the hackle was far too long in the barb; usually when the hackle is broad so is the web in the butt end of the hackle stalk. I found a lady breeder who had some Red Jungle Fowl, mainly crossbreeds and I acquired a crossbred cock which I think was the result of Jungle Fowl to Old English Game partridge hen. Breeding this bird to my Old English game improved the shape and colour of my reds.

Old English Game black/red and gingers usually have hackles of an adequate shape, but in the greys, blues and the rest there is plenty of room for improvement from the fly-tyer's point of view.

The most interesting aspect of breeding for hackles on a small scale is not knowing what types are going to emerge from a nest of eggs. It is quite amazing how quality parents with well-shaped hackles can produce some throwbacks with soft and broad hackles which are nothing but utter rubbish – their capes are not even worth taking off. On the other hand you will have the occasional bird turn out such an unusual colour and quality that you will never see another like it.

When I was breeding I hatched all my chicks under broody hens and I do not have any experience with incubators – however I know my gamekeeper friend achieves over seventy percent with pheasant. I think with good management this sort of success ratio can be achieved with poultry, and it makes a breeding programme easier to plan, but acquiring broody hens at the right time can be difficult.

In recent years an increasing number of people have come into the hackle producing business. One of the reasons for this is the drying up of the commercial supply of capes from Asia. As the supply has got less so the prices have increased thereby making commercial hackle production a viable business. This supply of feathers from the east will decrease even further, thus opening the way for the hackle producing farms to increase their production and supply the fly-tyer with hackles of a colour and quality, in both cock and hen capes, that he has never before experienced.

When Carey Quarles of Colorado Quality Hackles began his quest to produce the ultimate quality hackle in the late 1970s he was fortunate to be able to obtain a selection of birds and eggs from Andy Miner, Jnr, the son of the late Andy and Nellie Miner of Minneapolis, Minnesota. Mr Miner, Snr, an avid fly-tyer and fisherman, had in the 1950s and 60s developed a quality strain of blue dun and other colours. It was these chickens that formed the foundation of Dr Quarles's investigation into poultry production for quality hackles.

In a letter to me Dr Quarles says: 'I was very lucky to have become friends with the late Andy Miner's wife. I had the pleasure of knowing her for the last six years of her life. She was such a lovely lady. She also gave me all of Andy's records and since I worked for a breeding company for ten years before coming to Colorado, I was able to understand what he did. For someone not having formal training in poultry, he was a genius in hackle breeding. I give him credit for the genetic Blue Dun that exists both at Colorado Quality Hackles and Herbert and Metz.'

Assembling his research team, Carey Quarles started his programme focusing on colour selection, feather selection, nutrition, breeding, housing, disease control, and areas in which growth and hackle quality could be improved; to complete the programme a leading geneticist was brought in to select the best possible mating crosses. A computer was used for setting up and recording the breeding programme.

The results of this intensive and high turnover breeding programme is that, after seven years of breeding, about 85 per cent of the colours can be predicted. Some of the colour lines produced breed true, white, black, furnace, brown, ginger, ginger variat, and some cree. All the other colours are made by crossing various colours to obtain the predicted colour. Badger, Furnace, and Cree can be produced by laying the various colours down over a two year period or by crossing certain colours. The pure white was produced over seven years; to produce this high quality white hackle it was necessary to use a very low selection percent to obtain pure white and all off-white colours had to be discarded each season; the capes usually run 87 per cent No 1 and No 2. Carey Quarles has put into practice the only possible method of producing high-quality hackles to enable the fly-tyer to acquire hackles of a colour which is correct for the pattern being dressed. He can purchase capes loaded with bright heavily feathered hackles with a minimum of web, fine strong flexible stems with even, short, fine diameter stiff barbs each side, bright gloss sheen and overall feather resiliency and strength. There is no doubt that Colorado Quality Hackles, with the start that Andy Miner's strain of poultry have given them, are well placed to meet any demand for hackles that may come their way.

One problem with breeding quality hackles is damage to plumage from feather pecking. A backward or sick bird is harried unmercifully and if not removed it will die. I always used to pen my young cockerals with an old master cock who kept order and stopped any fighting. When the birds start to develop their adult plumage, feather pecking can become a serious problem. Pecking at each other and tugging at each others feathers becomes a game, the hackles gripped are frayed or broken and even sometimes pulled out. Hackles treated in such a fashion are useless to the fly-tyer and where the hackles are pulled out the bird sometimes bleeds, the others will peck at the wound and cause great distress to the unfortunate bird. I used to split my cocks into separate coops before this problem started; Carey Quarles has designed new cages which does away with this problem and the cage design has minimized hackle damage. The only other option is debeaking or fitting plastic bits. A plastic bit is the easy option; it is a half moon shape with one side straight, with a gap in the curved side which allows the bit to be fitted. To fit the bit on the bird, carefully slide it over the upper mandible so that the two ends of the curved side clip into the nostril; when in position it lies between the top and bottom bills thus preventing the bill closing. This will stop the bird from gripping the other bird's hackles but it still can feed normally.

There is virtually no combination of colours that cannot be found in poultry particularly when crossing; it is this that makes breeding for hackles so fascinating. If it is not possible to acquire barred Plymouth Rocks or Old English Game for breeding, the following breeds may be available: Scots Grey, similar to the Plymouth Rock for colour, clean and defined barred plumage, the quality should be good and I cannot see any problems with hackle shape; the Leghorn is available in the following colours, white, black, brown, cuckoo (barred) and blue, the quality may vary quite considerably in the different colours but on the whole I think it should be adequate; Wyandotte are available in a wide range of colours, however quality may be suspect and stock should be checked but colour on the whole I think will probably be adequate.

To check the various breeds visit local poultry shows, talk to the breeders. If all goes well you will be soon on the way producing your own hackles which brings us back to what I said in the beginning of this book, there cannot be many fly-tyers who have killed a trout on a fly dressed with a hackle they have bred themselves.

14

Preparation of Bird Skin

For the enthusiast the skinning of small animals and birds for their fur or plumage to use in fly dresing, is just an extension of their sport and interest. Except for large animal skins which are best left for the professional tanner the amateur can easily tackle the following procedure.

Whether you are removing a whole skin or just a cape the technique is the same. To remove a skin from a cock pheasant, first pull the tail feathers and clip off the wings close to the body. Turn the bird onto its back and make an incision in the throat just below the beak. With a sharp knife or sharp pointed scissors cut straight down from the bottom of the breast to the tail, remove the feet at the first joint and make an incision up the inside of the leg joint, peeling the skin off the legs back to the tail and up over the bird's rump.

Turn the bird over so that it is now lying on its breast. Carefully pull the skin up over the back, cutting any membrane that does not come away easily. Gently pull the skin up past the wing stumps and peel carefully out over them; continue peeling, snipping the membrane where necessary, until the head is reached; the skin will now have to be cut away from the head until completed.

Pin the skin (feathers downwards) on the board starting from the head, keeping even pressure so the skin is taut but do not over stretch; when the skin is completely pinned out, dry it with tissue paper, peel off any membrane and trim any fat that can be easily removed. The skin now should be relatively clean with perhaps a little fat still attached, which will dry up.

Keep the skin in a dry warm place; every couple of days wipe it with tissue paper; after four or five days remove from the board and leave it to dry naturally. If the skin is soiled with blood wash it out with cold water and rinse it well. Place it between sheets of newspaper until dry. Do not dry it at too high a temperature otherwise the skin will curl at the sides and become hard. Once dry, trim the ragged edges and store away. Some writers recommend sprinkling borax on the skin; personally I do not bother as I find it keeps well enough naturally. When dealing with rabbit or any small mammal the easy method of drying the skin, after skinning the animal, is to turn the skin inside out and stuff it full of newspaper. It will dry out like this quite well. When dry, remove the newspaper and trim the skin so that it can be stored flat.

To remove the skin of a rabbit, first make an incision in the rabbit's abdomen and remove the intestine completely. Peel the skin back from each side of the body until your fingers meet at the back. Making sure all the skin at the back is free from the body now pull it off the back legs. Once the skin is clear of the back legs pull it towards the head up over the shoulders freeing the chest and front legs. It will be necessary to use a sharp knife to take the skin off the head. This is all that needs to be done; cure the skin in the manner that has already been described.

Storing fur and feather on the skin does make for more accurate selection of materials when tying and it does save time and avoids any mess. When I take a skin from a cock where the cape and saddle cape are the same colour, I will take them off in one piece. Some saddle hackles make splendid dry flies with plenty of turns for rough or fast water. Also in poultry look out for hackles on the cock's wings; very often there are some first class dry fly hackles to be had.

Glossary

Barb Fibres of a hackle.

Butt Where the tail and body join on a salmon fly.

Cheeks Hackles or feathers tied in short at the head of the fly.

Cape Hackles on the skin from neck or rump.

Dubbing needle Enables the fly-tyer to pick out fur from dubbed bodies thus giving the fly the shaggy dog look.

D.F.M. Daylight Fluorescent Material.

Drag Fly line caught in a fast current will form a belly in the line which will in turn speed up the flies, causing them to skate or drag.

Dapping Fishing bushy flies with a long rod by holding the rod with the tip up in the air and allowing the wind to lift and skip the fly on and off the surface of the water.

E.D. Treble Hook Long-shank treble hook on which very slim flies can be dressed.

Flying Treble Small treble hook joined by nylon line to the hook on which the fly is dressed thus forming part of the dressing.

Flashabou Very soft mobile plastic tinsel.

Hackle pliers A tool which enables the fly-tyer to hold the tip of the hackle and wind it around the hookshank.

Killer style wings Whole hackles from game birds and water fowl tied on each side of the hookshank.

Leader (Cast) Nylon line from end of fly line to the fly.

Married wing Strips of quill or shoulder feathers joined (married) together to form a multi-coloured feather wing.

Marabou Very soft fluffy mobile feather mainly from the turkey.

O.E.G. Old English Game.

Palmer hackled A hackle that is wound down the body of the fly.

Peal Young sea trout returning to the river for the first time.

Saddle hackle Hackle from a cock's back or saddle.

School peal Shoal of small sea trout.

Shooting head Short fly line attached to nylon backing (shooting line).

Skate Fly in a strong flow of water skidding on the surface.

Topping Golden pheasant crest.

Tube Fly A fly dressed on a narrow diameter tube.

Tag Tail of fly; could be a wool tag or in the case of the salmon fly, tinsel and floss wound on the hook-shank.

Wind slicks A strip of calm water cutting through the waves of the lake.

Web Barbules (little hooks) on the barbs causing each barb to stick to the one above it. The more barbules there are on the barbs of a hackle, the wider and further up the hackle is the web.

Waddington Fly A fly tied on a thin metal shank named after its inventor.

Wide Gape Albert Partridge 'wide gape' hook.

Whisks Fibres from hackles to form dry fly tails.